## Pioneers and Patriots of America.

By JOHN S. C. ABBOTT.

---

Each one volume, 12mo, illustrated, $1.50.

---

*DANIEL BOONE,*

*MILES STANDISH,*

*FERDINAND DE SOTO,*

*PETER STUYVESANT,*

*KIT CARSON,*

*DAVID CROCKETT.*

*Other Volumes in preparation.*

# KIT CARSON,

## THE PIONEER OF THE WEST.

BY

JOHN S. C. ABBOTT.

ILLUSTRATED.

NEW YORK:
DODD & MEAD, No. 762 BROADWAY.

*AMERICAN PIONEERS AND PATRIOTS.*

# CHRISTOPHER CARSON.

*FAMILIARLY KNOWN*

AS

# KIT CARSON.

BY

JOHN S. C. ABBOTT.

WITH ILLUSTRATIONS BY

ELEANOR GREATOREX.

NEW YORK:
DODD & MEAD, No. 762 BROADWAY.
1874.

NEWBURGH STEREOTYPE CO.

LANGE, LITTLE & CO.,
PRINTERS,
108 TO 114 WOOSTER STREET, N. Y.

# PREFACE.

It is a prominent object of this volume to bring to light the wild adventures of the pioneers of this continent, in the solitudes of the mountains, the prairies and the forests; often amidst hostile Indians, and far away from the restraints and protection of civilization. This strange, weird-like life is rapidly passing away, before the progress of population, railroads and steamboats. But it is desirable that the memory of it should not drift into oblivion. I think that almost every reader of this narrative will be somewhat surprised, in its development of the character of CHRISTOPHER CARSON. With energy and fearlessness never surpassed, he was certainly one of the most gentle, upright, and lovable of men. It is strange that the wilderness could have formed so estimable a character. America will not permit the virtues of so illustrious a son to be forgotten.

JOHN S. C. ABBOTT.

# CONTENTS.

PAGE

## CHAPTER XVI.

### *Recollections of Mountain Life.*



## CHAPTER XVII.

### *Frontier Desperadoes and Savage Ferocity.*



## CHAPTER XVIII.

### *The Last Days of Kit Carson.*



## CHAPTER XIX.

### *The Last Hours of Kit Carson.*

# CHRISTOPHER CARSON.

## CHAPTER I.

### *Early Training.*

Birth of Christopher Carson.—Perils of the Wilderness.—Necessary Cautions.—Romance of the Forest.—The Far West.—The Encampment.—The Cabin and the Fort.—Kit an Apprentice.—The Alarm.—Destruction of a Trading Band.—The Battle and the Flight.—Sufferings of the Fugitives.—Dreadful Fate of Mr. Schenck.—Features of the Western Wilderness.—The March.

CHRISTOPHER CARSON, whose renown as Kit Carson has reached almost every ear in the country was born in Madison county, Kentucky, on the 24th of December, 1809. Large portions of Kentucky then consisted of an almost pathless wilderness, with magnificent forests, free from underbrush, alive with game, and with luxuriant meadows along the river banks, inviting the settler's cabin and the plough.

There were then many Indians traversing those wilds. The fearless emigrants, who ventured to rear their huts in such solitudes, found it necessary ever to be prepared for an attack.

But very little reliance could be placed even in the friendly protestations of the vagabond savages, ever prowling about, and almost as devoid of intelligence or conscience, as the wolves which at midnight were heard howling around the settler's door. The family of Mr. Carson occupied a log cabin, which was bullet-proof, with portholes through which their rifles could command every approach. Women and children were alike taught the use of the rifle, that in case of an attack by any blood-thirsty gang, the whole family might resolve itself into a military garrison. Not a tree or stump was left, within musket shot of the house, behind which an Indian could secrete himself.

Almost of necessity, under these circumstances, any bright, active boy would become a skilful marksman. A small garden was cultivated where corn, beans and a few other vegetables were raised, but the main subsistence of the family consisted of the game with which forest, meadow and lake were stored. The settler usually reared his cabin upon the banks of some stream alive with fishes. There were no schools to take up the time of the boys; no books to read. Wild geese, ducks and other water fowl, sported upon the bosom of the river or the lake, whose waters no paddle wheel or even keel disturbed. Wild turkeys, quails, and pigeons at times, swept the air like clouds. And then there was the intense excitement of occasionally bringing down a deer, and even of shooting a ferocious grizzly bear or wolf or catamount. The romance of the sea creates a Robinson Crusoe. The still greater romance of the forest creates a Kit Carson. It often makes even an old man's blood thrill in his veins, to contemplate the wild and wondrous adventures, which this majestic continent opened to the pioneers of half a century ago.

Gradually, in Kentucky, the Indians disappeared, either dying off, or pursuing their game in the unexplored realms nearer the setting sun. Emigrants, from the East, in large numbers entered the State. Game, both in forest and meadow, became scarce; and the father of Kit Carson, finding settlers crowding him, actually rearing their huts within two or three miles of his cabin, abandoned his home to find more room in the still more distant West.

Christopher was then the youngest child, a babe but one year old. The wilderness, west of them, was almost unexplored. But Mr. Carson, at his blazing fireside, had heard from the Indians, and occasionally from some adventurous white hunter, glowing accounts of the magnificent prairies, rivers, lakes and forests of the far West, reposing in the solitude and the silence which had reigned there since the dawn of the creation.

There were no roads through the wilderness. The guide of the emigrants was the setting sun. Occasionally they could take advantage of some Indian trail, trodden hard by the moccasined feet of the savages, in single file, through countless generations. Through such a country, the father of Kit Carson commenced a journey of several hundred miles, with his wife and three or four children, Kit being an infant in arms. Unfortunately we are not informed of any of the particulars of this journey. But we know, from numerous other cases, what was its general character.

It must have occupied two or three weeks. All the family went on foot, making about fifteen miles a day. They probably had two pack horses, laden with pots and kettles, and a few other essential household and farming utensils. Early in the afternoon Mr. Carson would begin to look about for a suitable place of encampment for the night. He would find, if possible, the picturesque banks of some running stream, where there was grass for his horses, and a forest growth to furnish him with wood for his cabin and for fire. If the weather were pleasant, with the prospect of a serene and cloudless night, a very slight protection would be reared, and the weary family, with a buffalo robe spread on the soft grass for a blanket, would sleep far more sweetly in the open air, than most millionaires sleep in tapestried halls and upon beds of down.

If clouds were gathering and menacing winds were wailing through the tree-tops, the vigorous arm of Mr. Carson, with his sharp axe, would, in an hour, rear a camp which could bid defiance to any ordinary storm. The roof would be so thatched, with bark and long grass, as to be quite impenetrable by the rain. Buffalo robes, and a few of the soft and fragrant branches of the hemlock tree, would create a couch which a prince might envy. Perhaps, as they came along, they had shot a turkey or a brace of ducks, or a deer, from whose fat haunches they have cut the tenderest venison. Any one could step out with his rifle and soon return with a supper.

While Mr. Carson, with his eldest son, was building the camp, the eldest girl would hold the baby, and Mrs. Carson would cook such a repast of dainty viands, as, when we consider the appetites, Delmonico never furnished. It was life in the "Adirondacks," with the additional advantage that those who were enjoying it, were inured to fatigue, and could have no sense of discomfort, from the absence of conveniences to which they were accustomed.

If in the darkness of midnight, the tempest rose and roared through the tree-tops, with crushing thunder, and floods of rain, the family was lulled to sounder sleep by these requiems of nature, or awoke to enjoy the sublimity of the scene, whose grandeur those in lowly life are often able fully to appreciate, though they may not have language with which to express their emotions.

The family crossed the Mississippi river, we know not how, perhaps in the birch canoe of some friendly Indian, perhaps on a raft, swimming the horses. They then continued their journey two hundred miles farther west, till they reached a spot far enough from neighbors and from civilization to suit the taste even of Mr. Carson. This was at the close of the year 1810. There was no State or even Territory of Missouri then. But seven years before, in 1803, France had ceded to the United States the vast unexplored regions, whose boundaries even, were scarcely defined, but which were then called Upper Louisiana.

Here Mr. Carson seems to have reached a very congenial home. He found, scattered through the wilderness, a few white people, trappers, hunters, wanderers who had preceded him. The Indians, in numerous bands, as hunters and as warriors, were roving these wilds. They could not be relied upon, whatever their friendly professions. Any wrong which they might receive from any individual white man, their peculiar code of morals told them they might rightly attempt to redress by wreaking their vengeance upon any pale face, however innocent he might be. Thus hundreds of Indian warriors might, at any time, come swooping down upon Mr. Carson's cabin, laying it in ashes, and burying their tomahawks in the brains of his family.

The few white men, some half a dozen in number, who had gathered around Mr. Carson, deemed it expedient for self-defence to unite and build a large log cabin, which should be to them both a house and a fort. This building of logs, quite long and but one story high, was pierced, at several points, with portholes, through which the muzzles of the rifles could be thrust. As an additional precaution they surrounded this house with palisades, consisting of sticks of timber, six or eight inches in diameter, and about ten feet high, planted as closely as possible together. These palisades were also pierced with portholes.

With a practiced eye, these men had selected a very beautiful spot for their habitation, in what is now called Howard county, Missouri, just north of the Missouri river. It seems that they had much to fear from the Indians. There were at this time, frequent wars with them, in the more eastern portions of the continent, and the rumors of these conflicts reached the ears of all the roving tribes, and greatly excited them. It became necessary for the settlers to go upon their hunting excursions with much caution.

As the months passed rapidly away, other persons one after another, came to their fort. They were glad to find a safe retreat there, and were welcomed as giving additional strength to the little garrison. Game began to be scarce around their lonely habitation, for the crack of the rifle was almost incessantly heard there. It thus became necessary to resort more generally to farming, especially to raising large fields of corn, whose golden ears could easily be converted into pork and into bread. With these two articles of food, cornbread and bacon, life could be hilarious on the frontier. Keenness of appetite supplied the want of all other delicacies.

When they went to the cornfield to work, they first made a careful exploration of the region around, to see if there were any lurking savages near. Then with their guns ever ready to be grasped, and keeping a close lookout for signs of danger, they ploughed and sowed and gathered in their harvest.

Thus fifteen years passed away. Civilization made gradual encroachments. Quite a little cluster of log huts was reared in the vicinity, where the

HERALD

inmates in case of necessity could flee to the fort for protection. Christopher, at fifteen years of age, was an unlettered boy, small in stature, but very fond of the solitude of the forest, and quite renowned as a marksman. He was amiable in disposition, gentle in his manners, and in all respects a good boy. He had a strong character. Whatever he undertook, he quietly and without any boasting performed. With sound judgment, and endowed with singular strength and elasticity, he was even then deemed equal to any man in all the requirements of frontier life.

At a short distance from the fort there was a saddler, and Mr. Carson, with the advice of friends, decided to apprentice his son, now called Kit, to learn that trade. The boy remained in this employment for two weary years. Though faithful to every duty, and gaining the respect and confidence of his employer, the work was uncongenial to him. He longed for the freedom of the wilderness; for the sublime scenes of nature, to which such a life would introduce him; for the exciting chase of the buffalo, and the lucrative pursuits of the trapper, floating on distant streams in the birch canoe, and loading his bark with rich furs, which ever commanded a ready sale.

All these little settlements were clustered around some protecting fort. A man, who was brought up in the remote West, furnishes the following interesting incident in his own personal experience. It gives a very graphic description of the alarms to which these pioneers were exposed:

"The fort to which my father belonged was three-quarters of a mile from his farm. But when this fort went to decay and was unfit for use, a new one was built near our own house. I well remember, when a little boy, the family were sometimes waked up in the dead of night by an express, with the report that the Indians were at hand. The express came softly to the door and by a gentle tapping raised the family. This was easily done, as an habitual fear made us ever watchful, and sensible to the slightest alarm. The whole family were instantly in motion.

"My father seized his gun and other implements of war. My mother waked up and dressed the children as well as she could. Being myself the oldest of the children, I had to take my share of the burdens to be carried to the fort. There was no possibility of getting a horse in the night to aid us. Besides the little children we caught up such articles of clothing and provisions as we could get hold of in the dark, for we durst not light a candle or even stir the fire. All this was done with the utmost dispatch and in the silence of death. The greatest care was taken not to awaken the youngest child.

"To the rest it was enough to say *Indian*, and not a whisper was heard afterward. Thus it often happened that the whole number belonging to a fort, who were in the evening at their homes, were all in their little fortress before the dawn of the next morning. In the course of the next day their household furniture was brought in by men under arms. Some families belonging to each fort were much less under the influence of fear than others. These often, after an alarm had subsided, in spite of every remonstrance, would remove home, while their more prudent neighbors remained in the fort. Such families were denominated *fool-hardy*, and gave no small amount of trouble by creating such frequent necessities of sending runners to warn them of their danger, and sometimes parties of our men to protect them during their removal."

While Kit Carson was impatiently at work on the bench of the harness-maker, feeding his soul with the stories, often greatly exaggerated, of the wonders of scenes and adventures to be encountered in the boundless West, a party of traders came along, who were on the route for Santa Fe. This city, renowned in the annals of the West, was the capital of the Spanish province of New Mexico. It was situated more than a thousand miles from Missouri, and contained a mongrel population of about three thousand souls. Goods from the States could be readily sold there at a profit of one or two hundred per cent. Cotton cloth brought three dollars a yard.

Captain Pike, upon his return from his exploring tour, brought back quite glowing accounts of Santa Fe and its surroundings. It was a long and perilous journey from Missouri. The party was all strongly armed, with their goods borne in packs upon mules and horses. They expected to live almost entirely upon the game they could shoot by the way. Kit, purely from the love of adventure, applied to join them. Gladly was he received. Though but a boy of eighteen, his stable character, his vigorous strength, and his training in all the mysteries of frontier life, rendered him an invaluable acquisition.

The perils to which they were exposed may be inferred from the fate which some traders encountered soon after Kit Carson's party had accomplished the journey. There were twelve traders returning from Santa Fe. To avoid the Indians they took an extreme southern route. Day after day they toiled along, encountering no savages. It was December, and in that climate mild and serene. A caravan of twenty horses or mules travelling in single file, leaves a trail behind which can easily be followed.

Our adventurers were on a treeless prairie, an ocean of land, where nothing obstructed the view to the remote horizon. One beautiful morning, just after they had taken their breakfast and resumed their march, they perceived, not a little to their alarm, some moving object far in the distance behind. It soon resolved itself into a band of several hundred Indians, well mounted, painted and decorated in the highest style of barbaric art. They were thoroughly armed with their deadly bows and arrows and spears. It was indeed an imposing spectacle as these savage warriors on their fleet steeds, with their long hair and pennons streaming in the wind, came down upon them.

The little caravan halted and prepared for defence. There were twelve bold hearts to encounter several hundred foes on the open prairie. They knew that the main object of the Indians would be to seize the horses and mules and effect a stampede with their treasure. This being accomplished they would torture and murder the traders in mere wantonness. The savages had a very salutary caution of rifles which could throw a bullet twice as far as the strongest bow and the most sinewy arm could speed an arrow.

With the swoop of the whirlwind they approached until they came within gun-shot distance, when they as suddenly stopped. Each trader had fastened his horse or mule with a rope and an iron pin two feet long driven firmly into the ground. They knew that if they were captured a cruel death awaited them. They therefore prepared to sell their lives as dearly as possible. There was no trunk or tree, or stone behind which either party could hide. The open prairie covered with grass was smooth as a floor.

For a short time both bands stood looking at each other. The traders in a small group had every man his rifle. Had the Indians in their resistless strength come rushing simultaneously upon them, they could easily have been trampled into the dust. But it was equally certain that twelve bullets, with unerring aim, would have pierced the hearts of twelve of their warriors. The Indians were very chary of their own lives. They were never ready for a fight in the open field, however great might be the odds in their favor.

The savages having halted and conferred together, endeavored to assume a friendly attitude. With a great show of brotherly feeling they cautiously approached one by one. The traders not wishing to commence the conflict, began to move on, leading their animals and with their rifles cocked, watching every movement of the intruders. The mounted Indians followed along, quite surrounding with their large numbers the little band of white men.

Two of the mules lagged a little behind. One or two of the bolder of the savages made a dash at them and shot dead a man by the name of Pratt, who had them in charge. It was the signal of battle. A shower of arrows fell upon the traders, another man dropped dead, and an arrow buried its head in the thigh of another. Several of the Indians also fell. But the savages manifested a great dread of the rifle; and though they were forty to one against the white men, they retreated to a safe distance. As they felt sure of their victims, they did not wish to peril their own lives.

The traders hastily took the packs from the mules and piled them around for a barricade. The Indians were very wary. But by entirely surrounding the little fort and creeping through the long grass they succeeded in a few hours in shooting every one of the mules and horses of the traders. The savages kept up an incessant howling, and thirty-six dreadful hours thus passed away. It seemed but a prolongation of death's agonies. Hunger and thirst would ere long destroy them, even though they should escape the arrow and the tomahawk. It was not deemed wise to expend a single charge of powder or a bullet, unless sure of their aim. And the Indians crept so near, prostrated in the long grass, that not a head could be raised above the frail ramparts without encountering the whiz of arrows.

The day passed away. Night came and went. Another day dawned, and the hours lingered slowly along, while the traders lay flat upon the ground, cramped in their narrow limits, awaiting apparently the sure approach of death.

The night was dark, dense clouds obscuring the sky. The Indians themselves had become somewhat weary, and deeming it impossible for their victims to escape and feeling sure of the booty, which could by no possibility be removed, relaxed their watchfulness. As any death was preferable to captivity and torture by the Indians, the traders resolved, in the gloom of midnight to attempt an escape, though the chances were a hundred to one that they would be almost buried beneath the arrows of the howling savages.

Cautiously they emerged from their hiding-place, creeping slowly and almost breathlessly through the tall grass of the prairie, till quite to their surprise, they found themselves beyond the circle of the besiegers. There were ten men, one wounded, fleeing for life, expecting every moment to be pursued by five hundred savages. It was a long, dark, dismal winter's night, for in that changing clime a freezing night succeeded a sunny day. Like spectres they fled over the open prairie. That their flight might not be encumbered they had taken nothing with them but their guns and ammunition.

They were determined men. In whatever numbers and with whatever speed the mounted Indians might ride down upon them, ten of their warriors would inevitably bite the dust ere the fugitives could be taken. The Indians fully understood this. And when the morning dawned and they saw that their victims had escaped, instead of pursuing, they satisfied their valor in holding a triumphant powwow over the rich booty they had gained.

It was a chill day and the wind moaned dismally over the bleak prairie. But as far as the eye could extend no foe could be seen. Not even a tree obscured the vision. The exhaustion of the fugitives, from their thirty-six hours of sleeplessness and battle, and their rapid flight, was extreme. They shot a few prairie chickens, built a small fire of dried buffalo chips with which they cooked their frugal breakfast, and then. lying down upon the rank grass, slept soundly for a few hours.

They then pressed on their pathless way toward the rising sun. Through weary days and nights they toiled on, through rain and cold, sleeping often in stormy nights drenched, upon the bare soil, without even a blanket to cover their shivering frames. Their feet became blistered. Passing beyond the bounds of the open prairie, they sometimes found themselves in bogs, sometimes in tangled forests. There were streams to be waded or to be crossed upon such rude rafts as they could frame with their hatchets. Their clothes hung in tatters around them, and, most deplorable of all, their ammunition became expended.

For days they lived upon roots and the tender bark of trees. Some became delirious, indeed some seemed quite insane through their sufferings. The man who was wounded, Mr. Schenck, was a gentleman of intelligence and of refinement and of distinguished family connections, from Ohio. A poetic temperament had induced him to seek the romance of an adventure through the unexplored wilderness.

After incredible sufferings his wound became so inflamed that it was impossible for him to go any farther. Prostrate upon a mound in the forest his comrades left him. They could do absolutely nothing for him. They could not supply him with a morsel of food or with a cup of water. They had no heart even to bid him adieu. Silently they tottered along, and Mr. Schenck was left to die.

Through what hours of suffering he lingered none but God can tell. Not even his bones were ever found to shed any light upon his sad fate.

So deep became the dejection of these wanderers that often for hours not one word was spoken. They were lost in the wilderness and could only direct their steps toward the rising sun. After leaving Mr. Schenck there were but nine men remaining. They soon disagreed in reference to the route to follow. This led to a separation, and five went in one direction and four in another. The five, after wandering about in the endurance of sufferings which can scarcely be conceived of, fell in with a party of friendly Creek Indians, by whom they were rescued and treated with the greatest humanity. Of the other four two only succeeded in escaping from the mazes of the wilderness.

Such were the perils upon which the youthful Kit Carson was now entering from the pure love of adventure. He was not uninformed respecting these dangers. The knowledge of them did but add to the zest of the enterprise.

Crossing the plains of the interior of our Continent from the Missouri river to the Rocky mountains, was a very different undertaking half a century ago, from what it has been in more modern times. The route was then almost entirely unexplored. There were no charts to guide. The bold adventurers knew not where they would find springs of water, where forage for their animals, where they would enter upon verdureless deserts, where they could find fording-places of the broad and rapid rivers which they might encounter on their way.

This is not a forest-covered continent. The vast plains of the interior, whether smooth or undulating or rugged, spread far away for weary leagues, almost treeless. The forest was found mainly skirting the streams. Immense herds of buffaloes, often numbering ten or twenty thousand, grazed upon these rich and boundless pastures. Timid deer and droves of wild horses, almost countless in numbers, here luxuriated in a congenial home. There was scarcely a white man in the land whose eyes had ever beheld the cliffs of the Rocky mountains. And each Indian tribe had its hunting-grounds marked out with considerable precision, beyond which even the boldest braves seldom ventured to wander.

About a score of men started upon this trip. They were thoroughly armed, practiced marksmen, well mounted and each man led a pack mule, heavily laden with goods for the Santa Fe market. Their leader was commander-in-chief, whom all were bound implicitly to obey. He led the company, selecting the route, and he decided when and where to encamp.

The procession followed usually in single file, a long line.

Early in the morning, at the sound of the bugle, all sprang from their couches which nature had spread, and they spent no more time at their toilet than did the horse or the cow. After a hurried breakfast they commenced their march. Generally an abundance of game was found on the way. The animals always walked slowly along, being never put to the trot.

At noon the leader endeavored to find some spot near a running stream or a spring, where the animals could find pasture. The resting for a couple of hours gave them time for their dinner, which they had mainly picked up by the way.

An hour or two before sundown the camping ground was selected, the animals were tethered, often in luxuriant grass, and the hardy pioneers, by no means immoderately fatigued by the day's journey, having eaten their supper, which a good appetite rendered sumptuous, spent the time till sleep closed their eyelids in telling stories and singing songs. A very careful guard was set, and the adventurers enjoyed sound sleep till, with the dawn, the bugle call again summoned them. Under ordinary circumstances hardy men of a roving turn of mind, found very great attractions in this adventurous life. They were by no means willing to exchange its excitements for the monotonous labors of the field or the shop.

# CHAPTER II.

## *Life in the Wilderness.*

A Surgical Operation.—A Winter with Kin Cade.—Study of the Languages and Geography.—Return towards Missouri.—Engagement with a new Company and Strange Adventures.—The Rattlesnake.—Anecdote of Kit Carson.—The Sahara.—New Engagements.—Trip to El Paso.—Trapping and Hunting.—Prairie Scenery.—The Trapper's Outfit.—Night Encampment.—Testimony of an Amateur Hunter.

THE company of traders which Kit had joined enjoyed, on the whole, a prosperous expedition. They met with no hostile Indians and, with one exception, encountered nothing which they could deem a hardship. There was one exception, which most persons would deem a terrible one. The accidental discharge of a gun, incautiously handled, shattered a man's arm, shivering the bone to splinters. The arm rapidly grew inflamed, became terribly painful, and must be amputated or the life lost. There was no one in the party who knew anything of surgery. But they had a razor, a handsaw and a bar of iron.

It shows the estimation in which the firm, gentle, and yet almost womanly Kit Carson was held, that he was chosen to perform the operation. Two others were to assist him. The sufferer took his seat, and was held firmly, that in his anguish his struggles might not interfere with the progress of the knife. This boy of but eighteen years then, with great apparent coolness, undertook this formidable act of surgery.

He bound a ligature around the arm very tightly, to arrest, as far as possible the flow of blood. With the razor he cut through the quivering muscles, tendons and nerves. With the handsaw he severed the bone. With the bar of iron, at almost a white heat, he cauterized the wound. The cruel operation was successful. And the patient, under the influence of the pure mountain air, found his wound almost healed before he reached Santa Fe.

Having arrived at his journey's end, Kit's love of adventure led him not to return with the traders, by the route over which he had just passed, but to push on still further in his explorations. About eighty miles northeast of Santa Fe there was another Spanish settlement, weird-like in its semi-barbarous, semi-civilized aspects, with its huts of sun-baked clay, its Catholic priests, its Mexican Indians and its half-breeds. It was a small, lonely settlement, whose population lived mainly, like the Indians, upon corn-meal and the chase. Kit ever kept his trusty rifle with him. His gun and hatchet constituted his purse, furnishing him with food and lodging.

It was a mountainous region; here in one of the dells, Kit came across the solitary hut of a mountaineer by the name of Kin Cade. They took a mutual liking to each other. As Kit could at any day, with his rifle bring in food enough to last a week, the question of board did not come into consideration. It was in the latter part of November that Kit first entered the cabin of this hunter. Here he spent the winter. His bed consisted probably of husks of corn covered with a buffalo robe, a luxurious couch for a healthy and weary man. Pitch pine knots brilliantly illumined the hut in the evening. Traps were set to catch animals for their furs. Deer skins were softly tanned and colored for clothing, with ornamental fringes for coats and leggins and moccasins. Kit and his companion Kin were their own tailors.

Thus passed the winter of 1826. Both of the men were very good-natured, and of congenial tastes. They wanted for nothing. When the wind howled amid the crags of the mountains and the storm beat upon their lonely habitation, with fuel in abundance and a well filled larder, and with no intoxicating drinks or desire for them, they worked upon their garments and other conveniences in the warmth of their cheerful fireside. It is not hazarding too much to say that these two gentle men, in their solitary cabin, passed a far more happy winter than many families who were occupying, in splendid misery, the palatial residences of London, Paris and New York.

Kin Cade was perhaps a Spaniard. He certainly spoke the Spanish language with correctness and fluency. The intelligence of Kit is manifest from the fact that he devoted himself assiduously during the winter to the acquisition of the Spanish language. And his strong natural abilities are evidenced in his having attained, in that short time, quite the mastery of the Spanish tongue. It is often said that Kit Carson was entirely an uneducated man. This is, in one respect, a mistake. The cabin of Kin Cade was his academy, where he pursued his studies vigorously and successfully for a whole winter, graduating in the spring with the highest honors that academy could confer.

We ought not to forget that, in addition to the study of the languages, he also devoted much attention to the study of geography. They had no books, no maps. It is doubtful indeed, whether either Kit or his teacher could read or write. But Kin had been a renowned explorer. He had traversed the prairies, climbed the mountains, followed the courses of the rivers, and paddled over the lakes. With his stick he could draw upon the smoothly trodden floor of his hut, everything that was needful of a chart. There were probably many idle students in Harvard and Yale, who during those winter months did not make as much intellectual progress as Kit Carson made.

In the spring of 1827, Kit again went forth from his winter's retreat into the wilderness world, which has its active life and engrossing excitements, often even far greater than are to be found on the city's crowded pavements. Not finding in these remote regions any congenial employment, Kit decided to retrace his steps to Missouri. Most persons would have thought that the journey of some thousand miles on foot, through a trackless wilderness where he was exposed every step of the way, to howling wolves and merciless savages, a pretty serious undertaking. Kit appears to have regarded it but as an every-day occurrence.

He joined a party of returning traders. Much of the region they traversed may be aptly described in the language which Irving applies to Spain. "It is a stern melancholy country, with rugged mountains and long sweeping plains, indescribably lonesome, solitary, savage." After travelling nearly five hundred miles, about half the distance back to Missouri, they reached a ford of the Arkansas river. Here they met another party of traders bound to Santa Fe. Kit, who with great reluctance had decided to return home, eagerly joined them. His services were deemed very valuable, and they offered him a rich reward. His knowledge of the Spanish language became now a valuable investment to him, and as he had already twice traversed the route, he was at once invested with the dignity of guide as well as interpreter.

The following incident, related by a traveller who was passing over this same plain under the guidance of Kit Carson, shows that there are other dangers to be encountered besides the prowling savage and the wolf:

"It was a bright moonlight night. I had, as was my custom, spread my saddle leathers for a bed, and had drawn my blanket closely around me. Weary with the day's march, I had been sleeping soundly for several hours, when about midnight I awoke suddenly with an unaccountable feeling of dread. It must have been a sort of instinct which prompted me, for in a moment I was upon my feet, and then, upon removing my blanket, I found a rattlesnake, swollen with rage and poison, coiled and ready to strike.

"I drew away the blanket which served as a mattress, intending to kill the reptile, when to my astonishment it glided away making its escape into a small opening in the ground directly beneath my bed. The whole matter was explained at once. The snake had probably been out to see a neighbor; and getting home after I was asleep, felt a gentlemanly unwillingness to disturb me. And, as I had taken possession of his dwelling he took part of my sleeping place, crawling under the blanket where he must have lain quietly by my side until I rolled over and disturbed him. I can scarcely say that I slept much more that night, and even Carson admitted that it made him a little nervous."

Kit Carson was not a garrulous man. He was much more given to reflection than to talk, and he was never known to speak boastfully of any of his achievements. It is the invariable testimony of all who knew him, that he was mild, gentle and unassuming, one of Nature's noblemen. While travelling he scarcely ever spoke. Nothing escaped his keen eye. His whole appearance was that of a man deeply impressed with a sense of the responsibility of his office. He knew full well the treacherous character of the Indians, and that "the better part of valor is discretion."

He had often seen men killed at night by an invisible foe. From the impenetrable darkness which surrounded the camp fire, an arrow would come winged with death, piercing the heart of some mountaineer whose body was clearly revealed by the firelight. Kit Carson would never thus expose himself. He would always spread his blanket where the firelight would not reveal him.

"No, no boys," he would say to his often reckless comrades, "you may hang around the fire if you will. It may do for you, if you like it. But I do not wish to have a Digger Indian slip an arrow into me when I cannot see him."

A gentleman, who was guided over the plains by Kit, writes, "During this journey I have often watched Carson's preparation for the night. A braver man than Kit perhaps never lived. In fact, I doubt if he ever knew what fear was. But with all this he exercised great caution. While arranging his bed, his saddle, which he always used as a pillow, was disposed in such a manner as to form a barricade for his head. His pistols half cocked were placed above it, and his trusty rifle reposed beneath the blanket by his side, where it was not only ready for instant use but perfectly protected from the damp. Except now and then to light his pipe, you never caught Kit, at night, exposing himself to the full glare of the camp fire."

When on the march everything was conducted with military precision. At the early dawn as Kit gave the signal to prepare to start, all were instantly in motion. The mules were brought up; their packs were fastened firmly upon their backs, an operation which required much labor and skill. The mules have a strange instinct which leads them to follow with a sort of fascination a white horse. Thus generally a white horse or mare leads the cavalcade.

At times it was necessary to march long distances without meeting water. One of these dreary stretches was eighty miles long. It was necessary to pass over it as rapidly as possible, day and night almost without resting. In accomplishing one of these arduous journeys across a desert almost as bare as that of Sahara, the party set out one afternoon at three o'clock. One of the travellers writes:

"I shall never forget the impression which that night's journey left upon my mind. Sometimes the trail led us over large basins of deep sand, where the trampling of the mules' feet gave forth no sound. This, added to the almost terrible silence which ever reigns in the solitude of the desert, rendered our transit more like the passage of some airy spectacle where the actors were shadows instead of men. Nor is this comparison a strained one, for our way-worn voyagers, with their tangled locks and unshorn beards, rendered white as snow by the fine sand with which the air in these regions is often filled, had a weird and ghost-like look, which the gloomy scene around, with its frowning rocks and moonlit sands, tended to enhance and heighten."

It is said, as illustrative of Kit's promptness of action, that one night an inexperienced guard shouted "Indians." In an instant Kit was on his feet, pistol in hand. A dark object was approaching him. The loss of a second of time might enable a savage to bury his arrow-head deep in his side and to disappear in the darkness. Like a flash of lightning Kit fired and shot *his mule.* It was a false alarm.

The traders arrived safely in Santa Fe. Kit Carson, having faithfully performed his contract, began to look around for new adventures. Three hundred and fifty miles south of Santa Fe, there was the Mexican province of Chihuahua. It was a very rich mining district, and many adventurers had flocked to it from Spain. There was here a narrow valley of the Rio Grande about ten miles in extent, and quite well filled with the rude settlements of the miners. It is said that at one time there were nearly seventy thousand Spaniards and Indians scattered along the river banks in search of the precious metals.

A trading party was bound from Santa Fe to this region. Colonel Trammel was the leader of this party, and he eagerly secured the services of Kit

Carson, who, in addition to his experience as a traveller, could also perform the functions of an interpreter. We have no record of the incidents which occurred on this journey. As the route was well known, and there were no hostile Indians to be encountered, it was probably uneventful.

In this valley of El Paso, as it was called, Carson fonnd about five thousand people, mostly on the right bank of the river. The rudeness of the style in which they lived painfully impressed him. There was far more comfort in the cabins he had left in Missouri.

The houses were of clay baked in the sun, with earthen floors. Window glass was a luxury unknown. It seems almost incredible that they should have had neither chairs, tables, knives nor forks. These Mexicans were scarcely one remove from the untamed savages of the wilderness. Young Carson found nothing to interest him or to invite his stay. He returned to Santa Fe. The summer had now passed and another winter come.

About a hundred and fifty miles north of Santa Fe there was a small collection of huts called Taos, inhabited by trappers and hunters. This pursuit of game for food and fur was the employment which was congenial to him above all others. He directed his steps to Taos and at once entered into an engagement with Mr. Ewing Young, making his cabin headquarters.

Hunting and trapping were somewhat different employments, though perhaps equally exciting. The hunter depended upon his rifle, and was mainly in search of food. Still the robe of the buffalo and the coat of the grizzly bear were very useful in various ways, in the cabin of the hunter, and the softly tanned skin of the deer was invaluable, furnishing every article of clothing, shirt, leggins and moccasins. The skins of these animals had also a market value.

But the trapper was in pursuit of furs only. Though the men engaged in this pursuit were occasionally exposed to great hardship and suffering, still, in general they probably had, in the gratification of congenial tastes, a full share of such happiness as this world can furnish.

Young Carson, at the age of nineteen, had no taste for the scholarly seclusion of Yale or Harvard, no desire to stand all day behind the counter of the dry-goods store, or to work amid the crowd and the hum of the factory; he had no wish for what is called society, or to saunter down Broadway with his cigar and his cane, to exhibit his tightly-fitting garments; but he did love to set out on a hunting and trapping expedition. Let us follow him in one of these adventures.

It is a bright morning of the Indian summer, far along in November. There is a small log cabin on a mound of the wilderness. A dense forest breaks the northern winds. A rippling stream runs by the door. Beyond lies the prairie rich in verdure and enamelled with gorgeous autumnal flowers. Herds of buffalo are grazing in groups of hundreds, sometimes of thousands, on the broad expanse. Gangs of deer are seen, graceful, beautiful, following in the train of the antlered bucks, and with scent so keen and eyes so piercing that it requires the utmost skill of the hunter to approach them within rifle shot. Clouds of prairie chickens and quails are floating here and there in their short flight. It is the paradise of the hunter. Let no one think this description overdrawn. It would be difficult to exaggerate the loveliness of the flower-spangled prairie on a bright autumnal day. Eden could scarcely have presented scenes more attractive.

Young Carson stands at the door of the cabin with a stout mule before him. The animal is strong and plump, having been feasting upon the wild oats growing luxuriantly around. Carson is packing his mule. His outfit consists of a Mexican blanket, rough, thick and warm; a supply of ammunition; a kettle; possibly a coffee-pot and some coffee, which have been obtained at Santa Fe; several iron traps;

some dressed deerskin for replacing clothing and moccasins, a hatchet and a few other similar articles. In addition to his mule he may also take a pony to bear him on the way. Thus, if by accident, one give out, he has another animal to rely upon. And if very successful he may have furs enough to load them both on his return.

His costume consists of a hunting shirt of the soft and pliable deerskin, ornamented with long fringes and often dyed with bright vermilion. Pantaloons of the same material are also ornamented with fringes and porcupine's quills of various colors. Many a tranquil hour has been beguiled, in the long evenings and when the storm has beaten upon the hut, in fashioning these garments with artistic taste, learned of the Indians. A flexible cap, often of rich fur, covers his head, and moccasins, upon which all the resources of barbaric embroidery have been expended, cover his feet.

His rifle is borne on his left shoulder. His powder horn and bullet pouch hang under his right arm. In his bullet pouch he also carries spare flints, steel and various odds and ends. Beneath the broad belt which encircles his waist there is a large butcher knife in a sheath of buffalo hide. There is a whetstone in a buckskin case made fast to the belt, and also a small hatchet or tomahawk.

Thus accoutred, our young hunter and trapper sets out in search of the most lonely ravine which he can find among the mountains. He would reach if possible, some solitary stream which no white man's eye had ever beheld. He has no road, no trail to guide him. He rides his pony and leads his mule. Over the prairie, through the forest, across the streams, in silence and in a solitude which to him is not lonely, he passes on his way.

Night comes. If pleasant, he unburdens his horse and mule; drives his iron pickets into the ground, to which his animals are attached by ropes about thirty feet long, generally in pastures of rich grass or wild oats; builds a fire, cooks his supper, rolls himself in his blanket and sleeps soundly till morning. If the weather is unpleasant it makes but little difference. He knows exactly what to do. In a short time he constructs a frail but ample shelter; and then, with his feet towards the fire, sleeps sweetly regardless of the storm. His animals have no more need of shelter than have the bears and the buffaloes.

This is the *ordinary* life of the hunter. There are, of course, exceptions when calamity and woe come. A joint may be sprained, a limb broken. Fire may burn, or Indians may come, bringing captivity and torture. But the ordinary life of the hunter, gratifying his natural taste, has many fascinations. This is evidenced by the eagerness with which our annual tourists leave their ceiled chambers, in the luxurious cities, to encamp in the wilderness of the Adirondacks or the Rocky mountains. There is not a restaurant in the Palais Royal, or on the Boulevards which can furnish such a repast as these men often find, from trout which they have taken from the brook, and game which their own rifles shot, have cooked at the fires which their own hands have kindled. A gentleman who spent a winter in this way, in the green and sheltered valleys of the Rocky mountains, writes:

"There was something inexpressibly exhilarating in the sensation of positive freedom from all worldly care, and a consequent expansion of the sinews, as it were, of mind and body, which made me feel as elastic as a ball of India rubber, and in such a state of perfect ease that no more dread of scalping Indians entered my mind, than if I had been sitting in Broadway, in one of the windows of the Astor House. The very happiest moments of my life have been spent in the wilderness of the Far West, with no friend near me more faithful than my rifle, and no companion more sociable than my horse and mules.

"With a plentiful supply of pine logs on the fire, and its cheerful blaze streaming far up into the sky, illuminating the valley far and near, and exhibiting the animals, with well filled bellies, standing contentedly over their picket-pins, I would sit enjoying the genial warmth, building castles in the air. Scarcely ever did I wish to exchange such hours of freedom for all the luxuries of civilized life. Such are the fascinations of the life of the mountain hunter that I believe that not one instance could be adduced of even the most polished and civilized of men, who had once tasted the sweets of its attendant liberty and freedom from every worldly care, not sighing once more to partake of its pleasures and allurements.

"A hunter's camp in the Rocky mountains is quite a picture. It is invariably made in a picturesque locality. Nothing can be more social and cheering than the welcome blaze of the camp fire on a cold winter's night."

Young Carson, alone with his horse and mule, would journey from fifty to a hundred miles, examining every creek and stream, keeping a sharp lookout for signs of beaver. Having selected his location, generally in some valley eight or ten miles in extent, with a winding stream circling through the centre, which he had reason to believe was well stocked with beaver, he would choose a position for his camp. This would be more or less elaborate in its construction, according to the time he intended to spend there. But he would always find some sunny nook, with a southern exposure and a pleasing prospect, near the brook or some spring of sweet water, and, if possible, with forest or rock sheltering from the north winds.

In a few hours young Carson would construct his half-faced cabin, as the hunting-camp was called. A large log generally furnished the foundation of the back part of the hut. Four stout stakes were then planted in the ground so as to inclose a space about eight feet square. These stakes were crotched at the ends, so as to support others for the roof. The front was about five feet high, the back not more than four. The whole slope of the roof was from the front to the back. The covering was made of bark or slabs and sometimes of skins. The sides were covered in a similar way. The whole of the front was open. The smooth ground floor was strewed with fragrant hemlock branches, over which were spread blankets or buffalo robes. In front of the opening the camp fire could be built, or on the one side or the other, in accordance with the wind.

Thus in a few hours young Carson would erect him a home, so cosey and cheerful in its aspect as to be attractive to every eye. Reclining upon mattresses really luxurious in their softness, he could bask in the beams of the sun, cirçling low in its winter revolutions, or gaze at night upon the brilliant stars, and not unfrequently have spread out before him an extended prospect of as rich natural scenery as ever cheered the eye. He had no anxiety about food. His hook or his rifle supplied him abundantly with what he deemed the richest viands. He knew where were the tender cuts. He knew how to cook them deliciously. And he had an appetite to relish them.

Having thus provided himself with a habitation, he took his traps and, either on foot or on horseback, as the character of the region or the distance to be traversed might render best, followed along the windings of the stream till he came to a beaver dam. He would examine the water carefully to find some shallow which the beavers must pass in crossing from shoal to deep water. Here he would plant his trap, always under water, and carefully adjust the bait. He would then follow on to another dam, and thus proceed till six traps were set, which was the usual number taken on such an expedition.

Early every morning he would mount his horse or mule and take the round of his traps, which generally required a journey of several miles. The captured animals were skinned on the spot, and the skins only, with the tails which the hunters deemed a great luxury as an article of food, were taken to the camp. Then the skin was stretched over a frame-work to dry. When dry it was folded into a square sheet, the fur turned inward and a bundle made containing from ten to twenty skins tightly pressed and corded, which was ready for transportation. These skins were then worth about eight dollars per pound.

After an absence of three or four weeks, young Carson would return with his treasures, often several hundred dollars in value, to the rendezvous of Mr. Ewing Young at Taos. Soon again he would set out on another similar expedition. Thus Carson passed the winter of 1827.

## CHAPTER III.

*Among the Trappers.*

The Discomfited Trappers.—The New Party Organized.—A Battle with the Indians.—Trapping on the Colorado.—March to the Sacramento.—The Friendly Indians.—Crossing the Desert.—Instinct of the Mule.—The Enchanting Valley of the Colorado.—The Mission of San Gabriel.—Vast Herds of Cattle.—The Mission of San Fernando.—Adventures in the Valley of San Joaquin.—The Meeting of two Trapping Bands.—Reasons for Kit Carson's Celebrity.—A Military Expedition.—The Indian Horse Thieves.—The Pursuit and Capture.

SOON after Carson returned to the cabin of Mr. Young from one of his trapping expeditions, a party of trappers came back who had set out to explore the valley of the Colorado, in pursuit of furs. At Taos they were west of the Rocky mountains, and the route which they were to take led them still farther in a northwest direction, a distance of three or four hundred miles. It was known that the region was full of roving Indians, and it was not doubted that the savages, if they saw any chance of overpowering the trappers, would do so, and seize their effects, which to the Indians would prove booty of almost inconceivable value. The rifle gave the trappers such an advantage over the Indian, with his bow and arrows, that they never hesitated, when upon the open plain in encountering almost any superiority of numbers.

This party of eighteen trappers, with their horses and heavily laden mules, had advanced but a few days' journey, over an almost unexplored region, when they fell in with a powerful tribe of Indians, who, after a little palaver, seeing their weakness in numbers and the richness of their treasure, attacked them with great fury. The Indians had adroitly selected a spot where they could fight Indian fashion, from behind trees and logs. The battle lasted a whole day. We are not informed how many of either party fell in the fray. But the Indians seemed to swarm around the trappers in countless numbers, and the white men were, greatly to their chagrin, driven back with the loss of several mules.

As the discomfited party returned with their tale of disaster, the ire of Mr. Young was raised. It is a comment upon the number of men then roving the wilderness, that Mr. Young was in a short time enabled to organize another party of forty men, to resume the enterprise. It was a motley collection of Spaniards, Americans, Mexicans and half-breeds. Proudly this powerful band, well armed, well mounted and with heavily laden pack mules, commenced its adventurous march, burning with the desire to avenge the insult which the previous expedition had encountered.

Mr. Young had learned highly to prize the capabilities of young Carson, and engaged him to take a prominent position in this company on its hazardous tour. After a march of about a hundred miles, they reached the region occupied by the Indians who had attacked and defeated the former band. The savages, flushed by success, were all ready to renew the conflict. Mr. Young himself was the leader of the party. The Indians, by their gestures and shouts of defiance, gave unmistakable evidence of their eagerness for the fight.

There was some little delay as both parties prepared for the deadly strife. Mr. Young, a veteran in the tactics of the forest, posted his men with great sagacity. He had forty, as we have mentioned, in all. Twenty-five of them he hid in ambush. With the other fifteen he cautiously advanced, and at length, as if alarmed, halted. The eminences all in front of them, seemed filled with the plumed warriors. The previous conflict had taught them the powers of the deadly rifle bullet. They kept at a respectful distance, never advancing unless protected by some tree or rock.

But there were hundreds of savages almost surrounding the little band, and making the hills and plains resound with the hideous war-whoop. When the trappers halted and began slowly to draw back, a deafening shout arose from the triumphant foe, and in a simultaneous charge they advanced, but still cautiously, not venturing near enough to discharge their arrows. They were thus drawn along into the trap. When fairly within rifle range, twenty-five unerring marksmen from their concealment, almost at the same instant, opened a death-dealing volley upon the surprised and bewildered warriors. The slaughter was terrible beyond anything they had ever, in their native battles, witnessed before. Twenty-five of their bravest warriors, for the bravest were in the advance, fell dead or severely wounded.

The Indians were thrown into an utter panic. The thunder, the lightning, and the death-bolts had come from they knew not where. With almost the rapidity of thought the rifles were again loaded and the whole united band rushed forward upon the Indians who were now flying wildly in all directions. Instinct taught them to perform all sorts of gyrations to avoid the bullets which pursued them. They made no attempt to rally, though many of their proud warriors were left behind lifeless, or struggling in the convulsions of death.

The power of the rifle was such that, in those

days, forty or fifty men never hesitated to engage a whole tribe, though it might number one or two thousand warriors. A man will fight with terrible persistence when he knows that defeat is inevitable death by torture. It is a thousandfold better to fall beneath the arrow, the tomahawk or the war-club, than to be consumed alive amid the jeers and tortures of yelling Indians inspired with demoniac instincts. Thus with the trapper it was always either victory or death.

These hostile warriors were punished with a severity never to be forgotten. The fugitives carried far and wide to other roving tribes the tidings of their disaster. The bold trappers proceeded on their way, encountering no more serious molestation. Smoke upon the distant hills indicated that their march was watched. If a trap was set at any distance from the night's encampment, it was pretty surely stolen. Or if a weary mule was left to recruit, a little behind, intending to bring him up in the morning, before the dawn he disappeared.

The whole party followed slowly down a tributary of the Colorado river, very successfully trapping upon the main stream and its branches, until they reached the head waters of the San Francisco river. They then divided, and Mr. Young with Carson and seventeen others proceeded several hundred miles farther west, to the valley of the Sacramento. Before setting out for this long journey, as it was uncertain what game they might find by the way, two or three days were devoted to hunting. The skins of three deer were converted into water tanks, which were without difficulty carried by the mules. They were induced to this caution because some friendly Indians had assured them that there was a great destitution of water by the way.

On their march they encountered a tribe of Indians in all their native wildness. They were very friendly though they had apparently never seen a white man before. Perhaps their friendliness was *because* they had never yet met any of the pale faces, from whom they subsequently suffered such great wrongs. These Indians presented remarkably fine specimens of the physical man. They were tall, erect and admirably proportioned. Their features were European, their eyes very full and expressive, and the dress of men and women simple in the extreme. They were all splendid horsemen, and often as they entered the camp at full speed on their spirited chargers, it seemed as though the steed and its rider, like the fabled centaur, were but one animal. Their bodies were painted and oiled so as to resemble highly polished mahogany.

The travellers found the information communicated to them by the friendly Indians to be true. For four days they travelled over a dreary, sandy waste, where there were neither streams nor springs. At the camping place each night there was given from the tanks, a small amount of water to each animal and man, but only enough to sustain life. A guard was set over the rest, for should any accident befall it the destruction of the whole party would be the probable consequence.

As they were toiling along the fifth day, painfully through the sand, the mules began to manifest a strange excitement. They pricked up their ears, snuffed the air, then began to rush forward with all the speed their exhausted strength would allow. The sagacious animals had scented water at the distance of nearly a mile. It was a clear running stream, fringed with grass and shrubs. When the first mule reached the water, the remainder were scattered for a great distance along the trail. Here the party encamped and remained for two days to recruit.

The bags of deerskin were again filled with water and the journey was resumed. The route still led over a similar barren region, where both man and beast suffered great privations from the want of water. On the fourth day they came in sight of the splendid valley of the great Colorado. It was with

3*

a thrill of delight that they gazed upon its verdure and its luxuriance, which were an hundredfold enhanced from the contrast with the dreary region which they had just traversed.

In their march of eight days through this barren and gameless region, their provisions had become quite exhausted. They chanced to come across some Indians from whom they purchased an old mare. The animal was promptly cut up, cooked and eaten with great gusto. They also obtained, from the same Indians, a small quantity of corn and beans. In the rich meadows of the Colorado our adventurers again found abundance. They spent a few delightful days here, feasting, trapping and hunting. The animals found, for them, a paradise in the luxuriant pastures of wild oats.

Again the journey to the west was resumed. The account we have of their movements is so meagre that it is impossible to follow with accuracy the route they traversed. They followed for some leagues a river, when suddenly its waters disappeared. They apparently sank beneath the surface of the quicksands. Still there were indications which enabled them to follow the course of the river, until finally it rose again above the surface, and in the open air flowed on to the ocean.

At length they reached the celebrated Catholic

Mission of San Gabriel, near the Pacific coast. The Mission was then in a flourishing condition. The statistics, published in 1829, indicate a degree of prosperity which seems almost incredible. More than a thousand Indians were attached to the Mission, and were laboring in its widely-extended fields, tending its herds and cultivating the soil. The poor Indians, who were often half starved upon the plains, found here light employment, shelter and abundant food. The statistics to which we refer, state that the Mission had seventy thousand head of cattle, four thousand two hundred horses, four hundred mules, and two hundred and fifty sheep.

These Missions, several of which were established in a line, within about fifty miles of the Pacific coast, belonged to the Spanish government, and were supported by the revenues of the crown. Animals multiplied with great rapidity upon those luxuriant and almost boundless prairies. They ranged sometimes, it was said, spreading out over a hundred thousand acres of wonderfully fertile pastures. There must of course, have been much guess-work in estimating the numbers of these vast herds, generally wandering unattended at their pleasure. But with such supplies of animal and vegetable food there was no fear of want. The indolent Indians consequently gathered around the Missions in great numbers. They were all fond of show, and not unwillingly became such christians as consists in attending the ceremonies of the church.

The Mission, with its buildings, cultivated fields and vast herds, seemed like the garden of Eden to our weary travellers. They however, remained here but one day, as they were not on a tour of pleasure but in pursuit of furs. A day's travel brought them to another but much smaller Mission, called San Fernando. Without any delay they pushed on towards the west, their object being to enter the valley of the Sacramento river, where they had been told that beavers could be found in great abundance. They expected to reach the banks of this now renowned, but then scarcely known river, after a few days' journey in a northeast direction. They were now in a delightful region. The climate was charming. Brooks of crystal water, and well filled with fishes, often crossed their path. There was abundant forage for their cattle ; and forest and prairie seemed alive with game.

They soon reached the banks of the San Joaquin, a lovely stream flowing northerly and emptying into the Sacramento near its mouth. There, finding a very eligible camping site, and many indications of beaver in the stream, Mr. Young halted his party, to rest for a few days, and in the meantime to set their traps. The general character of the scenery around them may be inferred from Mr. Bryant's description of a similar encampment in his overland journey to California.

"Finding here an abundance of grass, we remained the following day for the benefit of our animals. The valley was probably fifteen miles in length, with a variable width of two or three miles. It was a delightful spot. Wild plants grew in profusion, many-hued flowers studded its surface, and silvery streams, bordered by luxuriant verdure and shrubs, were winding through it. On both sides the mountains towered up by continuous elevations of several thousand feet, exhibiting a succession of rich vegetation, and then craggy and sterile cliffs, capped by virgin snow, the whole forming a landscape of rare combinations of the beautiful and sublime."

After a short rest the trappers continued their journey slowly, setting their traps on the San Joaquin and its tributaries. Pretty soon, much to their surprise, they saw indications that there was another band trapping on the same streams. In a short time they met, and it was found that the other party belonged to the Hudson Bay Company, and was commanded by Peter Ogden.

It is pleasant to record that the two parties, instead of fighting each other as rivals, cordially fraternized. For several weeks they trapped near together, often meeting and ever interchanging the courtesies of brotherly kindness. These men were from Canada. They were veterans in the profession of hunting and trapping, having long been in the employment of the Hudson Bay Company, and having served a regular apprenticeship to prepare them for their difficult aud arduous employment. Here again the peculiarity of Kit Carson's character was developed. Instead of assuming that he knew all that was to be known about the wilderness, and the business in which he was engaged, he lost no opportunity of acquiring all the information he could from these strangers. He questioned them very carefully, and his experience was such as to enable him to ask just such questions as were most important.

There is scarcely a man in America who has not heard the name of Kit Carson. No man can make his name known among the forty millions of this continent, unless there be something extraordinary in his character and achievements. Kit Carson was an extraordinary character. His wide-spread fame was not the result of accident. His achievements were not merely impulsive movements. He was a man of pure mind, of high morality, and intensely devoted to the life-work which he had chosen. His studies during the winter in the cabin of Kin Cade, had made him a proficient in the colloquial Spanish language. This proved to him an invaluable acquisition. He had also gathered and stored away in his retentive memory all that this veteran ranger of the woods could communicate respecting the geography of the Far West, the difficulties to be encountered and the mode of surmounting them. And now he was learning everything that could be learned from these Canadian boatmen and rangers.

Already young Carson had attained eminence. It was often said, "No matter what happens, Kit Carson always knows at the moment exactly what is best to be done."

Both as a hunter and a trapper, though he had not yet attained the age of manhood, he was admitted to be the ablest man in the party. And his native dignity of person and sobriety of manners commanded universal respect. In this lovely valley both parties lived, as trappers, luxuriously. They were very successful with their traps. And deer, elk and antelope were roving about in such thousands, that any number could be easily taken. These were indeed the sunny, festival days of our adventurers.

The two united parties, trapping all the way, followed down the valley of San Joaquin to the Sacramento. Here they separated. The Hudson Bay

Company set out for the Columbia river. Mr. Young and his party remained to trap in the valley of the Sacramento. At this time an event occurred which again illustrates the fearlessness, sagacity and energy of Kit Carson.

Not very far from their encampment there was the Catholic Mission of San Rafael. Some Indians belonging to that Mission, after committing sundry atrocities, fled, and took refuge in a distant Indian village. It was deemed important, in order that the Indians might be held under salutary restraint, that such a crime should not go unpunished. A force was sent to demand the surrender of the fugitives. But the Indians assumed a hostile attitude, refused to give up the criminals, and fiercely attacking the Mission party, drove them back with loss.

The Mission applied to the trappers for assistance. The request was promptly granted. Such a victory wonld puff up the Indians, render them insolent, and encourage them to make war upon other parties of the whites. Eleven volunteers were selected for the expedition, and the young and fragile Kit Carson was entrusted with the command. In manners he was gentle as a girl, with a voice as soft as that of a woman. He had no herculean powers of muscle, but he had mind, mental powers which had been developed in a hundred emergencies. And these

stout, hardy veterans of the wilderness seem with one accord to have decided that he was the fitting one to lead them into battle, where they were to encounter perhaps hundreds of savage warriors.

Cautiously Kit Carson led his little band so as to approach the Indian village unperceived. At a given signal they raised the war-whoop and impetuously charged into the cluster of wigwams. As the terrified warriors rushed out of the huts, all unprepared for battle, these unerring marksmen laid them low. One-third of the warriors were slain. The rest fled in dismay. The village was captured with the women and the children. The victorious Carson then demanded the immediate surrender of the criminals. The next day they were brought in, strongly bound, and delivered to the Mission. With his heroic little band Kit Carson returned to the encampment, apparently unconscious that he had performed any unusual feat.

The trappers purchased of the Mission sixty horses, paying for them in beaver skins, which always had a cash value. These horses were indispensable to the trapper. It required a large number to carry the packs of a successful trapping party. It would be impossible for the trappers to transport the packs upon their own backs. A party of forty trappers would need each a horse to ride. Then generally each man led a spare horse, lest the one he rode should break a limb or in any other way give out in the midst of the wilderness. If the expedition were successful, each trapper would have three or four horses or mules to lead or drive, laden with the packs of skins, the traps, camping utensils and a supply of food for an emergency. Thus a party of forty men would sometimes be accompanied by more than two hundred horses. Horses were cheap, and their food on the rich prairies cost nothing. But it was necessary to guard the animals with the greatest care, for the Indians were continually watching for opportunities to steal them.

Soon after Mr. Young, whose party it will be remembered now consisted of eighteen men, had made his purchase of horses, in preparation for a return, as the animals were feeding on the open prairie, a band of Indians succeeded one night in stealing sixty of them, and with their booty, like the wind they fled towards the valleys of the Snow mountains. Such a cavalcade of horses in one band, travelling over the turf of the prairie, would leave a trail behind which could easily be followed. The number of the Indian thieves was not known, though the boldness of the robbery and their tracks indicated that the band must have been large.

Twelve men were immediately detached to pursue the gang. Young Carson was then appointed leader. There were but fourteen horses left in the camp. Carson, having mounted his twelve men, had the other two horses led, to meet any emergency. Vigorously the pursuit was pressed. There was no difficulty in keeping the track. The Indian with all his cunning was never the equal of the far more intelligent white man. Indeed the ordinary savage was often but a grown up-child.

For more than one hundred miles Carson continued his pursuit before he came up with the robbers. They had already entered the green valleys of the Snowy mountains. The eagle eye of the pursuer saw some smoke circling up in the distance. No ordinary eye would have perceived it. Immediately he dismounted his men, and tethered the horses. The rifles were carefully examined, that every one might be loaded, primed, and in perfect order. The band then cautiously pressed forward, led by their boy captain, till they came to the entrance of a wild but lovely glen, where at the distance of perhaps a mile, they saw these savage warriors, enjoying all the luxury of a barbaric encampment. A mountain stream, rippled through the valley. The horses were grazing in the rich pasture. The thieves had killed six of the fat young horses, and having cooked them and feasted to utter repletion, were lounging around, basking in the sun, in the fullness of savage felicity. Little were they aware of the tempest of destruction and death about to burst upon them.

The Indians could not have chosen a more delightful spot for their encampment and their feast. Neither could they have selected a spot more favorable for the unseen approach of the pursuers. But the savages, having accomplished more than a hundred miles, deemed themselves perfectly safe.

Carson carefully reconnoitred the position, gave minute directions to his men, and they all, with the noiseless, stealthy movement of the panther, worked their way along until they were within rifle distance of their foes. Every man selected his victim and took deliberate aim. The signal was given. The discharge was simultaneous. Twelve bullets struck twelve warriors. Most of them dropped instantly dead. Almost with the rapidity of thought the rifles were loaded, and the little band rushed upon the bewildered, terror-stricken, bleeding savages. The Indians scattered in every direction. Eight were killed outright. Carson had no love of slaughter. Many more, in their flight, might have been struck by the bullet; but they were allowed to escape. All the horses were recovered excepting the six which the Indians had killed.

Great was the rejoicing in the camp when the

victorious party returned so abundantly successful. One of the annalists of this extraordinary man speaking of the enterprise, very truthfully writes:

"Carson, though at that day a youth in years and experience, had risen rapidly in the estimation of all, and had excited the admiration and enlisted the confidence of the entire band. When called upon to add his counsel, concerning any doubtful enterprise, his masterly foresight and shrewdness, as well as clearness in attending to details, gave him willing auditors.

"But it was the modest deportment he invariably wore, which won for him the love of his associates. Kit Carson's power in quickly conceiving the safest plan of action in difficult emergencies, and his bravery, which in his youth, sometimes amounted to rashness, caused his companions to follow his leadership. His courage, promptitude, self-reliance, caution, sympathy and care for the wounded, marked him at once as the master mind. Like the great Napoleon, when he joined the army for his first campaign, he was a hero, in spite of his youth, among men grown grey with experience."

The highest style of manhood, the most attractive character is that in which the mildness and the delicacy of the woman is combined with the energy and the fearlessness of the man. In Kit Carson we witness a wonderful combination of these two qualities. An acquaintance of the writer, who spent many years of his early life roving through the wilderness of the far West, and who had often met Kit Carson, said he never heard an oath from his lips. Even the rude and profane trappers around him could appreciate the superior dignity of such a character.

Rev. Dr. Bushnell, speaking of the region in which our trappers were engaged, says, "Middle California, lying between the head waters of the two great rivers, and about four hundred and fifty or five hundred miles long from north to south, is divided lengthwise parallel to the coast, into three strips or ribbons of about equal width. First the coastwise region comprising two, three, and sometimes four parallel tiers of mountains, from five hundred to four thousand, five thousand or even ten thousand feet high. Next, advancing inward we have a middle strip, from fifty to seventy miles wide, of almost dead plain, which is called the great valley; down the scarcely perceptible slopes of which from north to south, and south to north run the two great rivers, the Sacramento and the San Joaquin, to join their waters at the middle of the basin, and pass off to the sea. The third long strip or ribbon is the slope of the Snowy mountain chain which bound the great valley on the East, and contains in its foot-hills, or rather its lower half, all the gold mines."

It was in this middle region called The Great Valley, that Mr. Young and his trappers pursued their vocation. They commenced far south, at the head waters of the San Joaquin, and trapped down that stream, a distance of about one hundred and fifty miles. They then struck the greater flood of the Sacramento, and followed up that stream nearly three hundred and fifty miles. They had now obtained furs enough to load down all the horses and mules at their disposal. They prepared to return to Santa Fe, where they were sure of a ready market for their furs, which would be sent to Europe for their final sale.

## CHAPTER IV.

### *Conflicts with the Indians.*

The American Trapper.—The Trapper of the Hudson's Bay Company.—The Return Trip.—Polished Life in the Wilderness.—The Spanish Gentlemen.—Council of the Trappers.—Self-possession of Kit Carson.—The Camp Cleared of Intruders.—Robbing the Robbers.—Sale of the Furs.—Mr. Fitzpatrick's Expedition.—Pains and Pleasures of Rocky Mountain Life.—Pursuit of Indian Horse Thieves.—Extraordinary Battle.

IN the last chapter we have alluded to the friendly meeting, in the valley of San Joaquin, of the American trappers with a party from Canada, sent out by the Hudson's Bay Company. It is a remarkable fact, but one which all will admit, that the Hudson's Bay Company maintained far more friendly relations with the Indians than the Americans secured. In fact, they seldom had any difficulty with them whatever. The following reasons seem quite satisfactorily to explain this difference. It is said:

"The American trapper was not like the Hudson's Bay employees, bred to the business. Oftener than any other way he was some wild youth who, after some misdemeanor in the society of his native place, sought safety from reproach or punishment in the wilderness. Or he was some disappointed man, who with feelings embittered towards his fellows, preferred the seclusion of the forest and mountain. Many were of a class disreputable everywhere, who gladly embraced a life not subject to social laws. A few were brave, independent and hardy spirits, who delighted in the hardships and wild adventures their calling made necessary. All these men, the best with the worst, were subject to no will but their own. And all experience goes to prove that a life of perfect liberty is apt to degenerate into a life of license.

"Even their own lives, and those of their companions, when it depended upon their own prudence, were but lightly considered. The constant presence of danger made them reckless. It is easy to conceive how, under these circumstances, the natives and the foreigners grew to hate each other, in the Indian country, especially after the Americans came to the determination to "shoot an Indian at sight."

"On the other hand, the employees of the Hudson's Bay Company were many of them half-breeds, or full-blooded Indians of the Iroquois nation, towards whom nearly all the tribes were kindly disposed. Even the Frenchmen, who trapped for this Company, were well liked by the Indians on account of their suavity of manner, and the ease with which they adapted themselves to savage life. They were trained to the life of a trapper, were subject to the will of the Company, and were generally just and equitable in their dealing with the Indians. Most of them also had native wives, and half-breed children, and were regarded as relatives. There was a wide difference."

It was the month of September when Mr. Young and his party set out on their return. The homeward route was essentially the same which they had already traversed. They made a brief visit at the Mission of San Fernando, and then pressed on to the flourishing Mission village of Los Angelos. This City of the Angels, as it was called, from the salubrity of the climate and the beauty of the scenery, was on a small river about four hundred and fifty miles southeast from the present site of San Francisco.

Here Mr. Carson was introduced to a scene of refined and polished life, such as he had never witnessed before. He was informed that a Spanish gentleman of wealth was residing, at the distance of a few miles, on one of the most highly cultivated farms in the country. Young Carson, who never allowed any opportunity of extending his knowledge to escape him, dressed himself carefully in his best apparel, mounted a fine horse, well caparisoned, and set out to pay the Spaniard a visit.

He reached the *ranche*, as the farm was called, dismounted at a wicket gate, and having fastened his horse, walked up several rods, over a gravelled-walk, and beneath an avenue of trees, with occasional clumps of shrubs and flowers, until he reached the residence. It consisted of a spacious one story edifice, built of sun-baked bricks, called *adobe*. The dwelling was a hundred feet long, and the roof was rendered impenetrable to rain, being covered with a thick coating of asphaltum, mingled with sand. There was a spring of this valuable pitchy substance near the village; and the roofs of all the houses in Los Angelos were similarly covered.

A huge brass knocker was attached to the door. In response to its summons, an Indian girl made her appearance, and ushered him into an elegantly furnished parlor. There were several guitars lying about, with other indications that there were ladies in the household. Soon the gentlemanly owner of the farm appeared, in morning gown and slippers. He was a fine looking man, of dignified address, and courteously he saluted the stranger.

There was a native air of refinement about Kit Carson, with his highly intellectual features, and his modest, self-possessed bearing, which seemed always to win, at sight, interest and confidence. Carson introduced himself as an American, though he spoke in the Spanish language. His host, evidently much pleased with his guest, replied in English, saying:

"I address you in your native tongue, which I presume is agreeable to you, though you speak very good Spanish."

The parties were immediately on the most friendly terms. Carson sought information which the Spanish gentleman was able and happy to give. It was an early hour in the morning. Carson was invited to remain to breakfast, and was soon conducted to the breakfast-room, where he was introduced to the wife of his host, and several sons and daughters.

There was no restraint in conversation, as both parties could speak, with equal apparent facility, the Spanish and the English. There was a young gentleman from Massachusetts, a graduate from a New England college, who was private tutor in the family. After breakfast the stranger was conducted around the farm, and to the vineyard.

"I have more grapes," said the host, "than I know what to do with. Last year I made more butts of wine than I could dispose of, and dried five thousand pounds of raisins. I have travelled through Europe, and I think that neither the valley of the Rhine nor the Tagus can produce such grapes as ours.

I think that the Los Angelos grape is indeed food for angels. They are equal to the grapes of Eschol. You remember the heavy clusters that were found there, so that two men carried one on a pole resting upon their shoulders. See that vine now. It is six inches in diameter. And yet it needs a prop to sustain the weight of the two clusters of grapes which it bears."

"I have more oranges," he said, "than I can either use or give away. This is the finest country the sun shines upon. We can live luxuriously upon just what will grow on our own farms. But we cannot get rich. Our cattle will only bring the value of the hides. Our horses are of little worth, for there are plenty running wild, which a good huntsman can take with a lasso. I think that we shall have the Americans with us before many years, and, for my part, I hope we shall. The idea of the Californians generally, as well as other Mexicans, that the Americans are too shrewd for them, is true enough. But certainly there is plenty of room for a large population, and I should prefer that the race that has most enterprise should come and cultivate the country with us."

Thus the conversation continued for two hours. Young Carson modestly suggested that it would be better if the Spaniards were less cruel in breaking in their horses.

"Your horses," said he, "would make excellent buffalo hunters with proper training. I have some horses at camp, that I intend shall see buffalo. But why do you not deal gently with them when they are first caught? You might thus preserve all the spirit they have in the herd. Pardon me, but I think that in taming your horses you break their spirits."

"I sometimes think so too," the Spanish gentleman replied. "We mount one just caught from the drove, and ride him until he becomes gentle from exhaustion. Our custom is brought from Spain. It answers well enough with us, where our horses go in droves; and when one is used up, we turn him out and take up another."

When young Carson took his leave, the Spaniard, with true Castilian courtesy, pressed his hand, thanked him for his visit, and promised to return it at the camp. It was thus instinctively that Kit Carson, naturally a gentleman, took his position among gentlemen.

In the meantime most of the rude trappers, seeming to be almost of a different nature from Kit Carson, were indulging in a drunken carouse at Los Angelos. They got into a brawl with the Mexicans. Knives were drawn, wounds inflicted, and one Mexican was killed.

It became necessary to get these men away as

soon as possible. Carson was sent forward a day's march, with all who could be collected. The next day Mr. Young followed, having with much difficulty gathered the remainder of the band. Soon the party was reunited, and the men were recovered from their shameful debauch. Then for nine days they vigorously continued their march homeward, when they again reached the banks of the Colorado river, not far from the spot where they had crossed it before.

Here they encamped for a few days, while most of the men ranged the stream for many miles up and down, still very successfully setting their traps. Carson, with half a dozen men, was left to guard the camp. It was a responsible position. Nearly all the horses were there, and all the treasures of furs which they had gathered in their long and laborious excursion. As the animals were turned out to graze, the packs, which were taken from them, were arranged in a circular form so as to enclose quite a space, like a fortress. These bundles of furs not even a bullet could penetrate. Thus Kit Carson reared for himself and men a rampart, as General Jackson protected his troops with cotton bags at New Orleans.

Scarcely was this work completed, when a band of five hundred Indians was seen approaching. As usual, they stopped at a short distance from the fortified camp, and a few of the warriors, laying aside their arms and expressing by words and gestures the utmost friendliness, came forward and were admitted into the camp. They were followed by others. Soon there were enough stalwart savages there easily to overpower, in a hand-to-hand fight, the feeble garrison of but six men. Carson's suspicions were excited, and watching their movements with an eagle eye, he soon discovered that they all had concealed weapons.

Without the slightest apparent alarm he quietly summoned his men, with their rifles, into one corner of the enclosure. Then in his usual soft voice he directed each man to take deliberate aim at some one of the prominent chiefs. He himself presented the muzzle of his rifle within a few yards of the head of the leader of the now astonished and affrighted party. This was all the work of a moment. Then calmly he said to the leader, "leave this fort instantly or you are dead men." A moment of hesitation on their part, a word of parleying would have been followed by the simultaneous discharge of the rifles, and six of the warriors at least, would have been numbered with the dead. In a moment the fort was cleared, and the savages did not stop until they had got beyond the reach of rifle bullets.

One of these Indians could speak Spanish. Thus

Kit Carson again found the inestimable advantage of his winter's studies in the cabin of Kin Cade. The Indians, five hundred in number, might easily, at the expense of the loss of a few lives, have overpowered the white men, and seized all their animals and their goods. But Carson well knew their habits, and that they would never hazard a contest where they must with certainty expect a number of their own warriors to be slain. Friendly relations were opened with the Indians, only two or three being admitted to the fort at a time. The animals were tethered in the rich herbage within the protection of their rifles and were carefully watched, night and day.

In a few days the men who had left the camp on a trapping expedition, returned. The whole united company then followed down the south bank of the Colorado, setting their traps every night, until they reached its tide waters. From that point they struck over east to the river Gila, and trapped up the western banks of that river until they reached the mouth of the San Pedro, a distance of more than two hundred miles.

Their animals now were very heavily laden with furs, and they were in great need of more beasts of burden. The following is the account which is given of the manner in which they obtained a supply. It

4*

certainly looks very suspicious. It is not improbable that the Indians, had they any historians, would give a very different version of the story.

"Near the mouth of the San Pedro river they discovered a large herd of horses and mules. On a closer examination they found that they were in possession of a band of Indians, who had formerly given them some of their gratuitous hostilities. Not having forgotten their former troubles with these people, they determined to pay them off in their own coin by depriving them of the herd. A short search sufficed to discover the Indian camp. Without waiting an instant, they put their horses to their speed, and charged in among the huts. The Indians were so completely taken by surprise, that they became panic-struck, and fled in every direction. They however rallied somewhat and a running fight commenced, which lasted some time, but which did not change matters in favor of the Indians. The entire herd fell into the possession of the trappers.

"On the same evening, after the men had wrapped themselves up in their blankets, and laid down for sleep, and while enjoying their slumbers, a noise reached their ears which sounded very much like distant thunder. But a close application of the sense of hearing showed plainly that an enemy was near at hand. Springing up, with rifle in hand, for generally in the mountains a man's gun rests in the same blanket with himself, on all sleeping occasions, they sallied forth to reconnoitre, and discovered a few warriors driving along a band of at least two hundred horses. The trappers comprehended instantly that the warriors had been to the Mexican settlement in Sonora, on a thieving expedition, and that the horses had changed hands, with only one party to the bargain. The opportunity to instil a lesson on the savage marauders was too good to be lost.

"They saluted the thieves with a volley from their rifles, which, with the bullets whizzing about their heads and bodies, so astonished them that they seemed almost immediately to forget their stolen property, and to think only of a precipitous flight. In a few moments the whites found themselves masters of the field and also of the property. To return the animals to their owners was an impossibility. Mr. Young, therefore, selected as many of the best horses as he needed for himself and men, and, game being very scarce, killed two, and dried most of the meat for future use, turning the remainder loose."

Such were the morals of the wilderness. Mr. Young resolved himself into a court, of which he was legislator, judge, jury and executioner. The property of others he could confiscate at pleasure, for his own use. The Indians probably retaliated upon the first band of white men which came within their power. And this retaliation would be deemed an act of wanton savage barbarism demanding the extinction of a tribe.

Continuing their march up the Gila river, trapping all the way, from its head waters they struck across the country to Santa Fé. Here they found a ready market for their furs, at twelve dollars a pound. Their mules were laden down with two thousand pounds. Thus the pecuniary results of the trip amounted to the handsome sum of twenty four thousand dollars. The trappers, flush with money, returned to Taos. The vagabonds of the party soon squandered their earnings in rioting, and were then eager to set out on another excursion. It was now April, 1830.

Young Carson was at this time a very handsome young man of twenty-one years. He had obtained a high reputation, and his pockets were full of money, with which he scarcely knew what to do. It is said that, for a time, he was led astray by the convivial temptations with which he was surrounded. To what length he went we cannot ascertain. There is no available information upon this point. Perhaps the whole story is but one of those slanders to which all men are exposed. One of his annalists writes:

"Young Kit, at this period of his life, imitated

the example set by his elders, for he wished to be considered by them as an equal and a friend. He however passed through this terrible ordeal, which most frequently ruins its votary, and eventually came out brighter, clearer and more noble for the conscience polish which he received. He contracted no bad habits, but learned the usefulness and happiness of resisting temptation; and became so well schooled that he was able, by the caution and advice of wisdom founded on experience, to prevent many a promising and skilful hand from grasping ruin in the same vortex."

In the fall of this year Kit joined another trapping expedition. Its destination was to the innumerable streams and valleys among the Rocky mountains. Mr. Fitzpatrick, a man of good reputation and a veteran trapper, had charge of the party. Crossing a pass of the Rocky mountains, they pursued their route in a direction nearly north, a distance of about three hundred miles, till they reached the head waters of the Platte river. They were now on the eastern side of those gigantic ranges which form the central portion of the North American Continent.

Here, in the midst of the mountains, the winter was inclement, with piercing blasts and deep snows. Still the trappers, warmly clad, vigorously pursued both hunting and trapping, availing themselves of every pleasant day. In inclement weather they gathered joyously around their ample camp-fires, finding ever enough to do in cooking, dressing their skins, repairing garments, making moccasins, and in keeping their guns and knives in order. Some of these valleys were found sheltered and sunny. Even in mid-winter there were days of genial warmth. They occasionally changed their camp and trapped along the banks of the Green, the Bear and the Salmon rivers.

During the winter one sad incident occurred. Four of the trappers who were out in pursuit of game, were surrounded and overpowered by a numerous party of Blackfeet Indians, and all were killed. There were buffaloes in abundance in that region, and these animals found ample forage, as they had the range of hundreds of miles, and instinct guided them to sheltered and verdant glens. But in some of the narrow, wind-swept valleys the animals of the trappers suffered from exposure and want of food. They were kept alive by cutting down cottonwood trees and gathering the bark and branches for fodder. But the trappers themselves, having abundance of game, fared sumptuously.

The beaver is so intelligent that he is one of the most difficult animals in the world to entrap. Marvellous stories are told by the hunters of his sagacity. Many of the Indians believe that the beavers have human intelligence. They say that the only difference between the beaver and the Indian, is that the latter has been endowed by the Great Spirit with capabilities to catch the former.

Among these bleak, barren, gigantic ridges there are many lovely valleys to be found, scores of miles in length and width. Here are found two extensive natural parks, of extraordinary beauty. Apparently no landscape gardener could have laid them out more tastefully. There are wide-spread lawns, sometimes level as a floor, sometimes gently undulating, smooth, green and at times decorated with an almost inconceivable brilliance of flowers. Here and there groves are sprinkled, entirely free from underbrush. There are running streams and crystal lakelets. Birds of brilliant plumage sport upon the waters. Buffaloes, often in immense numbers, crop the luxuriant herbage. Deer, elks and antelopes bound over these fields, reminding one of his childish visions of Paradise. In the streams otter and beaver find favorite haunts.

During the winter, as business was a little dull, Kit Carson and four of his companions set off on a private hunting expedition. They were gone about six weeks. Soon after their return, in the latter part of January, a party of Crow Indians, one very dark night, succeeded in stealthily approaching the camp and in driving off nine of the animals which were grazing at a short distance. It was not until morning that the loss was discovered.

As usual Kit Carson was sent, at the head of twelve men, in pursuit of the thieves. They selected their best horses, for it was certain that the Indians would make no delay in their flight. It was found quite difficult to follow their trail, for, during the night, a herd of several thousand buffaloes had crossed and recrossed it, quite trampling it out of sight. Still the sagacity of Carson triumphed, and after being baffled for a short time, he again with certainty struck the trail.

For forty miles the pursuit was continued with much vigor. The horses then began to give out. Night was approaching. Carson thought it necessary to go into camp till morning, that the horses might be refreshed and recruited. There was a grove near by. Just as they were entering it for their sheltered encampment, Kit Carson saw the smoke of Indian fires at no great distance in advance of him. He had no doubt that the smoke came from the encampment of the party he was pursuing.

The Indians had fled from the north. Of course it would be from the north that they would look for the approach of their pursuers. The southern borders of their camp would consequently be less carefully guarded. The trappers remained quietly in their hiding-place until midnight. They then took a wide circuit, so as to approach the Indians from the south. The savages seemed to have lost all fear of pursuit, for the gleam of their triumphal fires shone far and wide, and the shouts of their barbaric revelry resounded over the prairie.

Very cautiously Carson and his men approached, availing themselves of every opportunity of concealment, creeping for a long distance upon their hands and knees. Having arrived within half gunshot they gazed upon a very singular spectacle, and one which would have been very alarming to any men but those accustomed to the perils of the wilderness.

A large number of Indian warriors, painted, plumed and decorated in the highest style of savage taste, were celebrating what they deemed a victory over the white men. Their camp was in a beautiful grove, on what would be called an undulating prairie. There was some broken ground which facilitated the approach of the trappers. The nine horses they had stolen were tethered in some rich grass, at a short distance from the encampment. The Indians had erected two large huts, or wigwams, which, in their caution, they had constructed partially as forts into which they could retreat and protect themselves should they be attacked.

The large fires were burning hotly. At these fires they had roasted two horses, and had feasted to satiety. They were now dancing franticly around these fires, brandishing their weapons, shouting their rude songs of defiance and exultation, interspersed with occasional bursts of the shrill and piercing war-whoop. The savages outnumbered the trappers many to one. They were also armed with rifles and had learned how to use them skillfully. Thus, in view of a battle, the odds seemed fearfully against the trappers.

It was a dark night in January, and a piercing winter wind swept the prairie. Even savage muscles will get weary in the frenzied dance, and the continuously repeated war-whoop will exhaust the most stentorian lungs. Carson ordered his men to remain perfectly quiet in their concealment. As they had but a scanty allowance of clothing, they suffered much from the intense cold. Soon after midnight the savages threw themselves down around the fires and most of them were soon soundly asleep.

Kit Carson then, with five of his companions, cautiously crept towards the horses, drew out the picket-pins and led them a short distance to a place of concealment nearer their own camp. Several of the party were then in favor of returning, with their recovered property, as rapidly as possible. They would have several hours' advantage of the savages, and they thought it not advisable to provoke a conflict with foes outnumbering them, and who were also armed with rifles.

But Mr. Carson said, " our horses are exhausted. We cannot travel fast. We shall certainly be pursued. The Indians can judge from our trail how few we are in numbers. They are perfectly acquainted with the country. They can select their point of attack. With their large numbers they can surround us First they will shoot our horses. Then we shall be on foot and at their mercy. We now can take them by surprise. Our only safety consists in so weakening them, and appalling them by the vehemence of our attack, that they will have no heart to renew the conflict."

We do not profess to give Mr. Carson's precise words. These were his views. They were so manifestly correct that all, at once, fell in with them. The united party then again advanced, with rifles cocked and primed, towards the Indian camp. The trappers were in the shade. The recumbent forms of the sleeping Indians were revealed by the smouldering fires. When they were within a few yards of the foe, an Indian dog gave the alarm. Instantly every savage sprang to his feet, presenting a perfect target to these marksmen who never missed their aim. There was almost an instantaneous discharge of rifles and thirteen Indian warriors fell weltering in their blood.

The rest, thus suddenly awoke from sound sleep, witnessing the sudden carnage, and with no foe visible, fled precipitately to their forts. But the trappers instantly reloaded their pieces and, secure from harm, in the darkness, and behind the trees, struck with the bullet every exposed Indian, and five more fell. This was an awful loss to the Indians. Still they greatly outnumbered the whites. But they were caught in a trap. They had neither food nor water in their forts. Not an Indian could creep from them without encountering certain death.

Upon the dawn of day the Indians were able to ascertain that their foes were but few in number. As the only possible resort, which could save them from destruction, they decided to make a simultaneous rush, from the forts into the grove, and to take their stand also behind the protection of the trees. This would give them, with their superior numbers, the advantage over the trappers. They were good marksmen with the rifle, and were accustomed to that style of fighting. Mr. Carson was prepared for this movement. They made the rush, and they met their doom. Thirteen more warriors were struck down, either killed or severely wounded.

The Indians had now lost thirty-one warriors. Discouraged and appalled they retreated. The way was now clear for the return of Kit Carson. The savages made no attempts to obstruct their path. With all the horses which had been stolen, and without a man injured, this Napoleon of the wilderness re-entered the camp to be greeted by the cheers of his comrades.

# CHAPTER V.

## *Marches and Encampments.*

The Encampment Among the Rocky Mountains.—The Attempted Stampede.—Retreat and Pursuit by the Savages.—The Alarm.—Loss of the Horses.—Their Recovery.—Enterprise of Kit Carson.—Fight with the Indians.—The Litter for the Wounded.—Union of the two Trapping Parties.—Successful Return to Taos.—Carson joins a Trading Party.—Chivalric Adventures.—Attacked by Bears.

MR. FITZPATRICK, with his party of trappers, wandering to and fro, found himself at length encamped on the head waters of the Arkansas river, in the heart of the Rocky mountains, more than a thousand miles from the point where that majestic stream empties into the Mississippi. Their intercourse with the Indians had not been such as to secure friendly relations. Powerful tribes were around them, ready to combine for their destruction. The men were widely scattered in their trapping excursions, and but few were left here to guard the camp and the furs already taken.

It is impossible to trace with accuracy the course pursued by these different bands, neither is it a matter of any moment. Kit found himself at one time, left with but one man to guard the camp. He was fully conscious of his danger, and made every possible preparation for defence, should they be attacked. With food in abundance, loop-holes properly arranged, and a number of rifles ever ready loaded, no war-party, however numerous, could seize the fort without the loss of many of their men. And as we have said, the boldest of these warriors were never willing to expose themselves unprotected to rifle shot.

Neither of the men dared to venture far from their camp for game. Fortunately this was not necessary. Game existed in such abundance that, almost from the door of their fortification, they could shoot any quantity they needed. They always kept a careful guard. While one slept the other watched. For a month these two men were in this lonely position. At the end of that time Mr. Blackwell, one of the partners in one of these expeditions, arrived with fifteen fresh men, and a very thorough outfit. It was a joyful meeting, and the whole party, taking with them their furs, commenced a march to the Salt springs, near the head waters of the Platte river.

These adventurers had been but four days on their route, when one morning as they were breakfasting, the guard gave the startling cry of "Indians."

Every man was instantly on his feet, rifle in hand. The horses of the trappers were at but a short distance from the camp, turned loose to crop the grass, which was there scanty, wherever they could find it. But when Kit Carson was in a company nothing was ever left to chance. The animals were all carefully hobbled, a hind foot and a fore foot so bound together that they could not possibly run.

The Indians, on fleet horses, with flaunting pennons, hair streaming in the wind, and uttering demoniac yells, came down like the sweep of the tornado upon the animals. Their object was to cause a stampede, that is, to throw the animals into such a panic that they would break away from everything, and follow the Indian horses off into the boundless prairie. The trappers thus left without any steeds, would find pursuit impossible.

The movement was so sudden and so rapid that, though several shots were fired, but one Indian was struck. He fell dead upon the sod. One horse only was lost. One of the warriors, as he was passing by on the full run, succeeded in cutting the cord of a rearing, struggling steed, and the terrified animal disappeared with the mounted herd. Had it not been for the precaution of hobbling the horses, probably every one would have been lost in this attempted stampede. What is usually called good luck, is almost always the result of wise precautions. In reference to this adroit mode of horse-stealing adopted by the Indians, it is written:

"These stampedes are a source of great profit to the Indians of the Plains. It is by this means they deprive the caravans of their animals. The Comanches are particularly expert and daring in this kind of robbery. They even train horses to run from one given point to another, in expectation of caravans. When a camp is made which is nearly in range, they turn their trained animals loose, who at once fly across the plain, penetrating and passing through the camp of their victims. All of the picketed animals will attempt to follow, and usually succeed. Such are invariably led into the haunts of the thieves, who easily secure them.

"Young horses and mules are easily frightened. And, in the havoc which generally ensues, oftentimes great injury is done to the runaways themselves. The sight of a stampede on a grand scale, requires steady nerves to witness without tremor. And woe to the footman who cannot get out of the way when the frightened animals come along. At times, when the herd is large, the horses scatter over the open country and are irrecoverably lost.

A favorite policy of the Indian horse thieves is to creep into camp, cut loose one animal and thoroughly frighten him. This animal seldom fails to frighten the remainder, when away they all go with long ropes and picket-pins dangling after them. The latter sometimes act like harpoons, being thrown with such impetus as to strike and instantly kill a valuable steed from among the brother runaways. At other times the limbs of the running horses get entangled in the ropes, and they are suddenly thrown. Such seldom escape without broken legs or severe contusions, which are often incurable. The necessity of travelling on, without delay, renders it an impossibility to undertake the cure, when it might be practicable under other circumstances."

The next day the party of trappers travelled fifty miles, till they thought themselves beyond the reach of the hostile savages. Still they knew how stealthily their trail might be followed, and they were vigilant to guard against surprise. They selected, for their night's encampment, a beautiful spot upon the banks of a clear mountain stream, which emptied into the Arkansas river. They had there a smooth and verdant meadow, of limited extent, affording fine pasturage. Here the wearied animals were strongly picketed. There was also a grove, where they could obtain fuel and timber for such camp protection as they might require.

It was nearly dark when they reached this spot,

hungry and tired after the long journey of the day. But their camp-fires soon blazed brightly. Rich viands of choice cuts of venison and other game, were cooked by artistic hands. And the mountain springs afforded them cool and delicious water. With ravenous appetites they partook of a feast which any gourmand might covet. And then wrapped in their furs, and surrounded by the silence and solitude of the wilderness, with the whole wild scene illumined by their fires, they fell asleep. In accordance with invariable custom a careful guard was set.

They had one cause of solicitude, which to any person unfamiliar with mountain life would have been very serious; the place abounded with rattlesnakes. The whole region seemed to be a favorite rendezvous for these venomous reptiles. These mountaineers, however, had become so thoroughly acquainted with their habits, as to sleep in the midst of them without anxiety. In the night the rattlesnake seldom moves, in the daytime with his rattles he gives chivalric warning before he strikes with his fangs. Consequently it is not often that the trapper or the Indian is bitten.

Our travellers carefully examined the ground over which they reared their frail shelters, and then folded in their blankets or buffalo robes, experienced no solicitude. About midnight a faithful dog began to bark furiously. It was not doubted that the sagacious animal scented the approach of Indians. Every trapper was instantly on his feet, with his rifle in his hand. Their attention was immediately directed to the horses. The Indians were professional thieves, not murderers; they were in search of booty, not of revenge. And when they sought to take the lives of the trappers, it was merely as a necessary means for attaining their end of robbery.

It subsequently appeared that the Indians were undoubtedly near, and that the dog had not given a false alarm. The savages probably from their covert, saw that the animals were strongly tethered, and that the trappers were on the alert. Any attempt to stampede the horses, would expose them to the bullets of these unerring marksmen. They therefore withdrew, waiting for a more favorable opportunity. After an hour of watching, the trappers, about seventeen in number, having posted an extra guard, lay down again, but not for sleep. They expected every moment to see a band of mounted savages, perhaps several hundred in number, coming with the sweep of the whirlwind upon their horses, and yelling like demons, as they drove the terrified animals far away into the wilderness. The night, however, passed away without further disturbance.

As the morning dawned serene and cloudless upon them, all suspicions seem to have been dispelled. They replenished their fires, cooked their savory breakfast, and decided to remain for a day or two in their delightful encampment. The region abounded with the most desirable game, and it was thought that beaver might be found in the adjacent streams.

Kit Carson had a remarkably retentive memory, and a wonderful aptitude for comprehending the mazes of rivers, mountains, and valleys. He had very thoroughly studied the geography of these regions, and told his companions that at a distance of a few miles, there was a much larger stream than that upon which they were encamped; and that he had been informed that beaver were to be found there in abundance. There were two ways of approaching that stream; the shorter, but more difficult one, was by clambering over a mountain ridge several hundred feet high, and then descending into the valley beyond, through which the river flowed. The other and much longer route, was to follow down the small stream upon whose banks they were encamped, for several miles, until they reached its entrance into the larger river.

Four of the trappers, led by Kit Carson, undertook to cross this Rocky Mountain peak, and explore the valley beyond. They mounted four horses, laden with their traps, and other articles essential for a short trapping excursion. Probably the Indians, hidden in the distance, were with keen eyes watching every movement at the camp. Carson and his companions had been absent but about four hours, and others of the party were dispersed in search of game, when a large band of Indians, mounted on fleet horses, with flaunting pennons, and hair streaming in the wind, and making the cliffs resound with their yells, succeeded in liberating a large number of the horses, and with their booty, rapidly disappeared down the winding glen.

This all took place in almost less time than it has required to describe it. The hardihood and fearlessness of these hunters is signally manifest in the fact that four of these men instantly grasped their rifles, and springing upon four of the fleetest of their remaining horses, set out in pursuit of these savages, who outnumbered them ten to one. The narrowness of the glen was such, that the pursuers had the decided advantage over the spoil-encumbered pursued. They soon overtook them, and opened upon them a deliberate and deadly fire. One warrior fell dead from his horse. The others, imminently exposed to the same fate, with terror abandoned the drove they had captured, and soon disappeared in their rapid flight. The horses were all regained, and with them the victorious party returned to the camp, One of the men however was seriously wounded, having been struck by a bullet from one of the Indian warriors, several of whom were armed with rifles.

In the meantime, Carson and his companions, after surmounting great difficulties, reached the valley they sought, and to their disappointment, found no beaver there. Crossing the ridge had proved so difficult, that they decided to return by the more circuitous route of the two valleys. As they were riding along on their pathless way, they suddenly came upon four Indian warriors, evidently on the war-path; painted, plumed and armed in the highest style of military decoration. The four Indians instantly turned their horses and fled. The four trappers at once spurred on their steeds, and pursued them.

They were dashing on at their highest speed, when suddenly they found they had been led into an ambush. Sixty warriors came rushing upon them from behind the hill, where they had been concealed. The trappers had no time for deliberation. There was but one possible escape. It was to run the gauntlet. Bowing down to the necks of their horses, so as to expose their persons as little as possible to bullets or arrows, they urged their steeds to their utmost speed. The horses had an instinctive dread of the Indian. Sharing the alarm of their riders, they became frantic with terror, and needed no urging in their impetuous race. The Indians were often within sixty feet of their victims, and bullets and arrows flew thickly around the trappers. But both parties being on the fiercest run, and there being interposing obstacles of rocks, and shrubs, and trees, accurate aim was impossible. As the fugitives drew near their camp, the Indians relinquished the pursuit. One of the men had been struck by an arrow and wounded.

It was late in the afternoon when these heroic men were all re-assembled around the camp-fires, to recount the adventures of the day. With the sleeplessness of the preceding night, and the toil and peril which the rising sun had ushered in, they were all exceedingly exhausted. Still the consciousness that they were surrounded by a vigilant and powerful foe, rendered it necessary for them to adopt every precaution for their safety. They tethered their horses with very great care, near their camp. They prepared hasty ramparts which guarded every approach; and having established a very careful guard, sought that repose which all so greatly needed. The night passed without alarm.

At the distance of four days' march, there was another encampment of trappers, under Mr. Gaunt.

They decided as speedily as possible to join them. But the two wounded men found their wounds so inflamed that they could not travel. The trappers, accustomed to such exigencies, prepared for them litters very ingeniously constructed. They cut two flexible poles about twenty-four feet long. These were laid upon the ground, three feet apart, and a buffalo robe laid between them, strongly fastened on either side, so as to present a swinging hammock about six feet in length. This left at either end shafts about six feet long. Two mules or horses, of about the same size were selected as carriers. The ends of these shafts were attached to saddles, on each of the animals. Thus the patient was borne by a gentle, swinging motion, over the roughest paths.

In four days they reached Gaunt's camp. The whole united party set out for the lovely region to which we have before alluded, known as the Great Park. Here they found beautiful scenery, game in abundance, a delicious climate, rich pasturage for their animals, but no beavers. Other trapping parties had just preceded them, and emptied all the streams of their furs. For a week or two they wandered far and wide, setting their traps in vain. At length Kit Carson, weary of such profitless pursuits, took two chosen companions with him, and with the hearty good wishes of Mr. Gaunt and the remaining trappers, set out on an expedition on his own account.

He plunged directly into the very heart of the mountains, where game not being abundant he would be less likely to be annoyed by the savages. His experience and sagacity guided him safely and successfully. For several months these three men wandered about among these lonely streams, which even the Indian rarely visited. They found beaver in abundance, and loading down their animals with the well packed furs, set out on their perilous journey home. It was necessary for them to pass over miles of open prairie, where Indian bands were ever found pursuing buffalo, deer and other game. It would seem that a miracle only could preserve them from attack, and they were too few in numbers for a persistent defence.

The sagacity of Kit Carson, however, triumphed over all the obstacles he had to encounter. He traversed the forest and the prairie undiscovered, and reached Taos with all his animals and their precious freight. Here he found furs in great demand. Traders were there from various parts of the States, ready to purchase his supply at the highest prices. Kit Carson was abundantly rewarded for all his toil, and for a mountain trapper, might be deemed rich. His two companions speedily squandered their earnings in all kinds of extravagant and senseless revelry. Mr. Carson, having perhaps learned wisdom from past experience, judiciously invested the sums he had acquired.

Mr. Carson had now very decidedly stepped out from the ranks of vagabondage, in which so many of the reckless trappers were wandering, and had entered the more congenial association with intelligent and respected men. There was at that time at Taos, a gentleman by the name of Lee. He had the title of Captain, having been formerly an officer in the United States army. He was then a partner in the firm of Bent and Vrain, merchants of renown in the fur trade. This firm, in the eager pursuit for furs, had dispatched Captain Lee to these remote frontiers in New Mexico.

Bands of energetic trappers were penetrating streams and valleys, over distances thousands of miles in extent. Many of the Indians also, seeking lucrative trade with the white men, had purchased steel traps and had become quite successful in the capture of beavers. Captain Lee had obtained a large number of mules. These he was to load with packs, containing such goods as he thought would be the most eagerly sought for by the trappers. Then with a cavalcade of perhaps forty or fifty mules, horses for his party to ride, and spare horses to meet any accidental loss, he was to set out on a long tour of hundreds of miles, climbing the mountains, threading the valleys, crossing the prairies in search of these widely wandering bands.

In exchange for his goods he received furs; and the mules returned with their freightage of very rich treasure. This was in the latter part of October, 1832. Captain Lee became acquainted with Kit Carson, and immediately appreciated his unusual excellencies as a companion in an enterprise so arduous and perilous, as that in which he was engaged. He made him so liberal an offer to join his company, that Mr. Carson promptly accepted it.

There is a narrow mule-path which has been traversed for ages, between New Mexico and California. The mules and the Indians ever travel it in single file. It was then known by the name of The Old Spanish Trail.

As merchants, not trappers, they marched, without any delay, down White river, forded Green river, and struck across the country to Windy river. Ascending its windings, they reached the camp of Mr. Robidoux, who, with twenty men in his employ, was there setting his traps. They had scarcely arrived at the encampment, when snow began to fall, and an early winter seemed to be setting in. It was deemed expedient for the united party to establish winter quarters there. They erected very comfortable lodges, of buffalo skins, quite impervious to wind and rain, and made everything snug for a mountain home. They had food in abundance, ample materials for making and repairing their clothing, and when gathered around their bright and warm camp-fires seemed to be in want of nothing.

Attached to Mr. Robidoux's company there was an Indian of great strength and agility, in whom much confidence was reposed. He had become very expert with the rifle, and had shrewdly studied all the white man's modes of attack and defence. Horses were in this remote region very valuable. They could not easily be obtained, and were indispensable to transport the furs. They were worth two hundred dollars each.

This Indian, one night, selected six of the fleetest horses, and mounting one and leading the rest, with his stolen property, disappeared over the trackless waste. It was a sum total loss of twelve hundred dollars. But the immediate pecuniary loss was not all, for the horses could not easily be replaced, and without them all the movements of the trapping party were greatly crippled. Mr. Robidoux, knowing Kit Carson's reputation for sagacity and courage, immediately applied to him to pursue the Indian. It was just one of those difficult and hazardous enterprises which was congenial to the venturous spirit of Carson.

There was a friendly tribe of Indians in the vicinity, in which there was a young warrior whose chivalric spirit had won the confidence and regard of Carson. This young man was easily induced to join him in the chase. But a short time was required for preparation. Grasping their rifles, and taking their blankets, they each mounted a fine horse and set out in pursuit of the fugitive, who had several hours the start of them. The wary thief had so successfully concealed the direction of his flight that it took them some time to discover his trail. Having at length found it, they set off, at the highest speed which they felt that their animals could endure. Over soft ground, the marks left by six horses, running in one compact band, could be without difficulty followed. But at times the nature of the soil was such that but a very indistinct imprint of their footprints was left.

As the thief, in his flight, conscious that he might be overtaken, would make no difference between day and night, it was necessary that his pursuers should also press on without allowing darkness to delay them. This added greatly to the difficulty of following the trail. But the sagacity of Carson and his intelligent Indian comrade triumphed over all these obstacles. For one hundred miles they followed the fugitive with unerring precision. But now they encountered a serious calamity.

This singular race was down the valley of the Green river. The Indian's horse suddenly gave out completely. He could go no farther. Nothing remained for Carson but to relinquish the pursuit, and slowly to return with the dismounted Indian, or to continue the chase alone. Carson could not endure the thought of failure. His pride of character led him ever to resolve to accomplish whatever he should undertake. He seems not at all to have thought of the peril he would encounter in grappling with the savage alone. The Indian was of herculean size and strength, and of wonderful agility. He was well armed, and thoroughly understood the use of his rifle. His bravery had already given him renown, and it was certain that under the circumstances he would fight with the utmost desperation.

Kit Carson, on the other hand, was slender and almost boyish in stature. In a conflict with the burly savage it would be a David meeting a Goliath.

It was a peculiarity of Mr. Carson's mind, that his decisions were instantaneous. He never lost any time in deliberation; but whatever the emergency, he seemed instinctively to know at the moment, exactly the best thing to be done. The most mature subsequent deliberation invariably proved the wisdom of the course he had adopted. This was said to have been a marked peculiarity in the mind of Napoleon I. However great the complication of affairs, however immense the results at issue, his mind at a single flash discerned the proper measures to be adopted; and without the slightest agitation the decision was pushed into execution.

Carson looked for a moment upon his unhorsed comrade, uttered no words of lamentation, bade him good bye, wished him a successful return, and pushed forward on his truly heroic enterprise. Thirty miles farther he rode alone through the wilderness, carefully husbanding his horse's strength, allowing him occasional moments of rest, and not unfrequently relieving him of his burden as he ran along by his side. Though Mr. Carson was, as we have said, very fragile in form, his sinews seemed tireless as if wrought of steel.

At length, just as he was rounding a small eminence on the open prairie, he caught sight of the Indian with his stolen cavalcade, not an eighth of a mile before him. He was mounted on one of the most powerful of the steeds, moving leisurely along, leading the rest. There chanced to be two or three trees not far from the savage. The moment he caught sight of Carson, his keen eye discerned who his foe was. Instantly he leaped from his horse, rifle in hand, and rushed at his highest speed for the trees. Could he but reach that covert, Carson's fate was sealed beyond any possibility of escape. Sheltered by the trunk of the tree, he could take deliberate aim at his foe, exposed on the open prairie within half rifle shot.

Carson comprehended the peril of his position. He sprang from his horse, unslung his rifle, took calm and sure aim, and just at the moment when the Indian was reaching his covert, the sharp report was heard, the bullet whistled through the air, the Indian gave one convulsive bound and fell dead upon the sod. The savage had already cocked his rifle. As he fell the piece was discharged, and the bullet intended for Carson's heart, whizzed harmlessly through the air. Such scenes were of constant occurrence in this wild mountaineer life. They produced no lasting impression. The shooting of a bear, a buffalo or an Indian seemed about alike eventful. These pioneers being entirely beyond the protection of law, were compelled to be a law to themselves.

Mr. Carson collected the horses, who were all very weary, and quietly commenced his return home. He did not urge the animals at all, allowed them to feed abundantly on the rich prairie, and after a few days' journey, modestly entered the camp with his recaptured animals all in good condition. This was another of those victories which Carson was continually winning, and which were giving him increased renown.

A few days after his return to the encampment, two or three wandering trappers entered their lodges, and informed them that a numerous party were encamped on Snake river, about fifteen days' journey from them. This party was in the employ of two men quite distinguished in the fur trade, Messrs. Fitzpatrick and Bridger. Snake river is one of the tributaries of Green river, or rather flowing from the western declivities of the Rocky mountains, it first enters Bear river, then Green river, then the Colorado river, down whose current it flows a distance of more than a thousand miles into the gulf of California.

The encampment at Snake river was five or six hundred miles almost due north from Taos. West of the Rocky mountains the climate is much more mild than in the same latitudes east of those gigantic ridges. Though it was midwinter, and though many snow-storms were to be encountered, Mr. Lee decided to set out immediately on that journey, doubting not that he could readily dispose of his remaining goods to Messrs. Fitzpatrick and Bridger.

The execution of this enterprise would require a

very laborious march; but still one not fraught with much danger from the severity of the cold. Though there were often treeless prairies, whose bleak expanse they must traverse, all the streams, even the smallest, were fringed with forests. Suitable precaution would enable them every night to obtain the shelter of some one of these groves. They were almost certain during the day to obtain all the game they would need. A couple of hours' work with their axes, would enable them to rear a sufficient shelter for the night. With an immense fire roaring, and crackling, and throwing out its genial warmth in front of their camp, they could, wrapped in their furs and with their feet to the fire, enjoy all the comfort which the pioneers of the wilderness could desire. No matter how dismally the wintry storm might wail through the tree-tops, no matter how fiercely the smothering, drifting snow-storm might sweep the prairie, they, in their warm and illuminated cabins, could bid defiance alike to gale and drift. Their hardy animals, ever accustomed to unsheltered life in winter as well as summer, knew well how to find the grass beneath the snow, or to browse upon the succulent foliage.

The journey, though it proved very toilsome, was successfully accomplished. Captain Lee, with Carson, and their accompanying band, having reached the

Snake river encampment, readily sold all his goods, taking his pay in beaver skins. With his rich purchase packed upon the backs of his horses, he returned to Taos. As there was nothing in Captain Lee's journey home to require the services of so important a man as Mr. Carson, the latter decided to remain and unite himself with the trappers.

The party was large, the beavers were scarce, and after the lapse of a month Mr. Carson decided that the prospect of a rich remuneration in the distribution of their furs, was not encouraging. He therefore arranged an expedition on his own account. His popularity as a man and his reputation as a trapper were such that every man in the party was ready to join him. He selected three of the best men, and crossing the main ridge of the Rocky mountains, a distance of about one hundred and fifty miles, reached the Laramie river, a stream which flowed into the north fork of the Platte.

The warm airs of spring were now beginning to breathe through these valleys. On the Laramie and its tributaries, Carson and his companions continued trapping through the whole summer. They were successful beyond their highest expectations. As they were to carry their furs for sale to Taos, which was on the west side of the mountains, they set out, laden with their goods, to cross the wide and rocky range. It was slow work threading these defiles, and it required a journey of several days.

One afternoon having travelled for hours through a very dreary and barren ravine, in which they had found no game, they halted two hours before sunset. Carson, while his two companions were arranging the camp, set off with his rifle in pursuit of supper. He had wandered about a mile from the camp, when he came upon the fresh tracks of some elk. Following their trail for a little distance, he soon discovered a small herd of the beautiful animals grazing upon a hill-side, just on the edge of a grove. Moving with great care, circuitously he entered upon the covert of the trees, crept up within rifle range, selected the largest and fattest of the herd, and at the report of the rifle, the animal stood for a moment shivering as if struck by paralysis, and then dropped dead.

Carson was more than usually elated by his success. The party were all hungry. The region was extremely wild and barren, and there was great danger that they would have to go supperless to bed. Scarcely had the echo of his rifle shot died away, when Carson heard a terrific roar, directly behind him. Instantly turning his head, he saw two enormous grizzly bears, coming down upon him at full speed, and at the distance of but a few rods.

The grizzly bear is a larger animal and far more

ferocious, than the black bear. A bullet seems to prick rather than to maim him, and he will attack the hunter with the most desperate and persevering fierceness. Carson was helpless. He had discharged his rifle. The brutes were close upon him, and there were two of them. They could outrun him. His fate seemed sealed.

For once, Kit Carson was frightened ; but not so much so as in the slightest degree to lose his self-possession. With a lightning glance, his eye swept the grove, in search of a tree into whose branches he might climb. He saw one at a little distance, and rushed towards it, pursued by both of the monsters, growling and gnashing their teeth. With wonderful agility, he sprang and caught a lower branch, and drew himself up into the tree, just in time to escape the blow which one of the bears struck at him with his terrific claws. But he had by no means obtained a place of safety. He had been compelled to drop his rifle in his flight. The grizzly bear can climb a tree, far more easily than can a man. He was too far distant from the camp to hope for aid from that quarter. Again it seemed that a dreadful death was inevitable.

The bears hesitated for a moment, growling and showing their claws and their white teeth. Quick as thought Carson cut and trimmed from the tree a

stout cudgel, which would neither break nor bend. Soon, one of the bears commenced climbing the tree. The nose of the bear is very tender, and is the only point vulnerable to blows.

Cudgel in hand, Carson took his stand upon one of the branches, and as soon as the bear's head came within reach, assailed him with such a storm of blows, that he dropped howling to the ground. The other then made the attempt to climb the tree, and encountered the same fate. The blows which the sinewy arm of Carson had inflicted, evidently gave the animals terrible pain. They filled the forest with their howlings, and endeavored to bury their snouts beneath the sod. For some time they lingered around the tree, looking wistfully at their prey, as if loth to leave it. But they did not venture to incur a repetition of the chastisement they had already received. At length, with almost a ludicrous aspect of disconsolateness, they slowly retired into the forest.

Carson waited until assured that they had entirely withdrawn. He then descended the tree, reloaded his rifle, and repairing to the spot where he had shot the elk, found that it had already been devoured by wolves. This adventure had occupied many dreadful hours. It was not until the morning dawned, that Carson found his way back to his anxious companions in the camp. He often said that never in his life, had he been exposed to greater peril, than on this occasion.

## CHAPTER IV.

*The Rendezvous.*

Fair in the Wilderness.—The Encampment.—Dispersion of the Trappers.—Hostility of the Blackfeet.—Camp on the Big Snake River.—The Blackfeet Marauders.—The Pursuit.—The Calumet.—The Battle.—Kit Carson wounded.—The Rencontre with Shunan.—The Defeat and Humiliation of Shunan.—Remarkable Modesty of Carson.—Testimony to Mr. Carson's Virtues.

IN the morning the party fortunately found, in one of their traps, a beaver, upon whose not very palatable flesh they breakfasted. The tail of a beaver when well cooked, is esteemed quite a delicacy. But one tail would not furnish sufficient food for three men. Fifteen days passed away before Kit Carson's little band was re-united with the larger company of Messrs. Fitzpatrick and Bridger. A rendezvous had been appointed at a spot on Green river, which afforded great attractions for an encampment.

In some unexplained way intelligence had been conveyed, through the wilderness, to the widely dispersed trappers, that a Fair for trading, would be held at a very commodious and well-known spot on the above-mentioned stream. There was here a green, smooth, expanded meadow; the pasturage was rich; a clear mountain stream rippled through it, fringed by noble forest trees. The vicinity afforded an abundance of game. Here they reared their camps and built their roaring fires. Band after band of trappers and traders came in with loud huzzas. Within a few days between two and three hundred men were assembled there, with five or six hundred horses or mules.

On one of the gorgeous days of the Indian summer, the encampment presented a spectacle of beauty which even to these rude men was enchanting. There was the distant, encircling outline of the Rocky mountains, many of the snow-capped peaks piercing the clouds. Scattered through the groves, which were free from underbrush, and whose surface was carpeted with the tufted grass, were seen the huts of the mountaineers in every variety of the picturesque, and even of the grotesque. Some were formed of the well tanned robes of the buffalo; some of boughs, twigs and bark; some of massive logs. Before all these huts, fires were burning at all times of the day, and food was being cooked and devoured by these ever-hungry men. Haunches of venison, prairie chickens, and trout from the stream, were emitting their savory odors, as they were turned on their spits before the glowing embers.

The cattle, not even tethered, were grazing over the fertile plain. It was indeed a wild, weird-like, semi-barbaric Fair which was thus held in the very heart of the wilderness. Men of many nationalities were present, in every variety of grotesque costume; and not a few Indians were there, with scarcely any costume at all. For nearly two months the Fair continued, with comings and goings, while hill and plain often resounded with revelry.

At length the festival was dissolved, and the mountaineers, breaking up into smaller bands, separated. The traders, with their horses loaded down with the furs, returned to the marts of civilization. The trappers again directed their steps to the solitudes of the remoter streams.

Kit Carson joined a party of fifty men, to explore the highest tributaries of the Missouri river. The region was occupied by a numerous band of warlike Indians, called Blackfeet. Many of the warriors had obtained rifles. The itinerant trader could not refrain from furnishing the Indians with guns and ammunition, at the exorbitant prices which the savages were ready to pay. It shows the superiority of the white men, that fifty of them ventured to enter upon these plains and into these defiles, where thousands of these well-armed warriors were watching for their destruction.

The enterprise proved more bold than successful. The trappers found the Indians so vigilant and hostile, that it was necessary to protect themselves by an intrenched camp. They had to adopt the most wearisome precautions to protect their animals, never allowing them to graze beyond rifle distance from the camp, unless under a strong guard. Matters grew daily more and more desperate. The Indians seemed to be gathering from great distances, so as almost to surround the encampment. If any small party wandered a mile, to examine their traps, they were pretty sure to find the traps stolen, and to be fired upon from ambush. This state of affairs at length constrained them to quit the country. Like an army, exposed hourly to an attack from its foes, this heroic band of fifty men commenced its march in military array, watching with an eagle eye, knowing not but that at any moment hundreds of strongly mounted, well-armed savages might come rushing down upon them. They could indulge in no rest, till they got beyond the territory of the Blackfeet.

A march of one or two hundred miles brought them to the banks of the Big Snake river. It was the month of November. In those northern latitudes winter was setting in with much severity. The hill-tops were covered with snow; the streams were coated with ice; freezing blasts from the mountains swept the bleak plains and the narrow defiles. It was necessary to go into winter quarters for a couple of months. But there was no discomfort in this.

They selected a snug valley having a southern exposure, with a northern barrier of hills, and in the midst of a wide-spread grove which fringed a pure mountain stream. There were fifty men. Every man belonged to the working class. Every man was skilled in the trades of hunting, trapping, wigwam-building, cooking, and tailoring. A few hours' work reared their cosey huts. Fuel was cheap and abundant. The broadcloth for their clothing,was already woven on the backs of buffaloes, bears, deer and wolves. Their own nimble hands speedily formed them into garments impervious to wind and cold. They had laid in quite a store of game, which the cold weather preserved, and there was enough more within their reach. And fortunately for them all, nature's law of prohibition, had effectually banished from the whole region all intoxicating drinks. Where there is no whiskey there is rarely any quar rel. The pure mountain stream supplied them with their health-giving beverage.

In a few days everything was cosey and comfortable around them. During the months of December and January, and until the middle of February, while wintry blasts swept the hills, warmth, abundance and friendliness reigned in these sheltered, cheerful huts in a Rocky Mountain valley. There was one exciting event which disturbed the serenity of this winter encampment.

A band of Blackfeet Indians had cautiously dogged their footsteps, watching for an opportunity to stampede their horses. One very dark night, a number of these savages, supported by quite a numerous band of warriors, crept, like wolves, into the grazing ground of the horses, and succeeded in seizing eighteen of them, with which they made off rapidly towards their own country. The loss was not discovered until morning. After a few moments' deliberation it was decided that the valuable property must be recovered if possible, and the Indians chastised for such insolence.

The unanimous voice called upon Kit Carson to lead the enterprise, and to select his men. He took eleven. In a few minutes they were all mounted; a blanket their only baggage; their rifles and ammunition their only stores. The ground was covered with snow. These veteran mountaineers knew well when and how to spare their horses for a continuous pursuit.

The Indians being more numerous, having horses to lead, and with their steeds somewhat jaded with the long journey from their own country, could not travel as fast as their pursuers were able to do with their fresh animals. Still the savages had so much the start that it required fifty miles of sharp riding before they were overtaken. Fortunately for the pursuers, there had been recently a heavy fall of snow, so that the Indians were under the necessity of breaking a path. Their party was so large that the white men were furnished with a clearly marked, well-trodden trail. This toil through the snow, seems quite to have exhausted the strength of the horses of the Indians. They had been compelled to stop at noonday to refresh the animals. A spot had been selected on a hill-side, where the wind had blown away the snow, and where the horses found, for grazing, an abundance of succulent dried grass.

Suddenly, and probably not a little to their consternation, the twelve trappers, rounding an eminence on the full trot, appeared before them. Carson halted his troop to reconnoitre; for his foes were strongly posted and far out-numbered him. The savages, seeing the impossibility of immediately gathering and mounting their horses for flight, cunningly sent a flag of truce to solicit a parley. According to their custom, this flag consisted of one of their warriors advancing entirely unarmed, half-way to the opposing band. There he stopped, and folding his arms, waited for some one of the other party similarly weaponless, to come forward to confer with him.

These savage thieves manifested a degree of intelligence in their cunning, which was hardly to have been expected of them. Through their interpreter they assumed an air of perfect innocence, affecting great surprise that the horses belonged to the trappers, saying that they supposed that they had been robbing their hereditary foes, the Snake Indians.

"Nothing would induce us," said these barbarian diplomatists, "to commit any depredations upon our friends the white men."

Such barefaced falsehood did not, for a moment, deceive Kit Carson. But it was needful for him to move with great caution. The number of the Indians, their position, their weapons, and the nature of the ground upon which they had met, rendered the result of a battle very doubtful. It would not do for Carson to manifest the slightest trepidation, or the least doubt of his ability to recover the stolen property, and to chastise the marauders.

After some pretty severe questioning, he suggested that since they were friends, they should all meet in council unarmed, and smoke the calumet of peace. There are generally some points of honor, which will bind the most abandoned men. Such was the smoking of the pipe of peace with the savages. A large fire was built. The two parties met around it. The calumet was lighted, and passed around to each person present. Every one of the savages first puffed two whiffs, and the white men then did the same. This was the solemn pledge that there should be no treachery.

The council then commenced. Several of the Indian warriors made long and wordy speeches, with many protestations of friendship, but carefully avoiding any offer to restore the stolen animals. Mr. Carson listened patiently and made no response, until they had talked themselves out. He then simply replied, that he was very happy to learn that the Indians were friendly in their feelings toward the whites, and that the taking of the animals was a mistake. The trappers would therefore overlook the affair, and peacefully return home with the restored horses.

The Indian orators again began to chatter, branching off upon various points irrelevant to the question at issue. But Mr. Carson was in no mood to be drawn into a profitless palaver. To these eloquent speeches he made no response, but simply demanded the return of the horses.

The Indians began to bluster, to talk loud and to grow insolent. But Mr. Carson never allowed himself to lose his temper. A man in a passion seldom acts wisely. With calm persistence he said, "I can listen to no overtures of peace, until our horses are restored." Still the Indians hesitated to provoke a battle in which some of their warriors would undoubtedly fall. At length they sent out and brought in five of the poorest and most exhausted of the horses, saying that these were all that they could or would restore.

The trappers accepted this as a declaration of war. In a body they retired to seize their rifles and to submit the question to the arbitrament of battle. The savages also, with tumultuous howlings, rushed to grasp their guns. The battle immediately commenced, each party seeking the shelter of trees. But for the dread in which the savages stood of the powers of the white men, the advantages would have been in their favor ten to one. There were unerring marksmen on both sides. No one could expose himself to the aim of either party without almost certain death. Kit Carson and one of his companions, by the name of Markhead, were the foremost of the band of trappers, and they stood behind trees not far from each other. As Carson was watching the movements of a burly savage, who was endeavoring to get a shot at him, he saw another savage taking deliberate aim, from his concealment, at Markhead.

With the rapidity of thought Carson wheeled around, and at the same instant the bullet from his rifle pierced the heart of the savage and he fell dead. But there was another report, almost simultaneous with that from Carson's gun. A bullet whizzed through the air, touched the bark of the tree, behind which nearly the whole of Carson's body was concealed, and severed one of the sinews of his shoulder, shattering a portion of the bone. The blood gushed freely from the wound, and Carson fell, almost fainting, to the ground. With much difficulty his friends succeeded in bearing him off from the field, and in their rough kindness ministered to his wants.

This loss of Carson's guidance and arm was irreparable and fatal to the trappers. Still they continued the battle valiantly, holding the Indians at bay until night came. The night was bitter cold. The trappers could not light any fire, for it would surely guide the Indians to their retreat, and present them as fair targets to the bullets of the savages.

Disappointed as these bold men were, they had

the consolation of feeling that the wound of their leader had not passed unavenged. They were sure that several of the Indians had been killed and many wounded. Though they did not doubt that the Indians would still fight desperately in defence, they did not fear that they would venture to pursue and to attack the trappers where they could choose their own ground. The trappers therefore, bearing as tenderly as possible their wounded leader, commenced their return to the camp which they reached in safety. The savages, as it afterward appeared, fled as rapidly as possible in the other direction.

The adventure added to the reputation of Kit Carson. All admitted that it was to save the life of a comrade that he had imperilled his own. And no one doubted that, but for his wound, his sagacity would have triumphed over the savages, and that he would have brought back all the horses. It was immediately decided, in general council, that another expedition of thirty men, under Captain Bridger, should pursue and chastise the thieves. This well armed party vigorously followed the Indian trail for several days. But the savages had fled so rapidly, into distant and unknown parts, that they could not be overtaken. The trappers returned disappointed to their camp.

Spring was returning with its milder breezes and

its warmer sun. The time for the spring hunt had commenced. There were no hostile Indians in the vicinity to disturb the trappers. Success, surpassing their most sanguine expectations, attended their efforts. Every morning the trappers came in from their various directions laden with furs. All were elated with their extraordinary prosperity. There is the spring hunting and the fall hunting. But there is a period in midsummer when the fur is valueless or cannot easily be taken. Game was then abundant, camping was a luxury. This was the time selected by the traders for their Fairs in the wilderness. Here, as we have mentioned, there was exchange of the commodities needed in mountaineer-life, for the furs the trappers had taken during the autumn, winter and spring. There was at this time another rendezvous on Green river, where there was to be a renewal of the scenes of the past year.

Kit Carson very speedily recovered from his wounds. His perfect health and temperate habits caused a cure, which seemed almost miraculous. As we have mentioned, these mountaineers were beyond the limits of the laws. There was no governmental protection whatever. Every man was compelled to be his own protector, filling the threefold office of judge, jury and executioner.

The incident we are about to record would have

been highly immoral in any well-ordered community where law was recognized and could be enforced. And yet the same act occurring in the savage wilderness may have merited the high commendation which it universally received.

There was a fellow at the rendezvous, as the Fair among the mountains was called, known as captain Shunan. He was of unknown nationality, of very powerful frame, a bully and a braggadocio. Totally devoid of principle, and conscious of his muscular superiority, he was ever swaggering through the camp, dealing blows and provoking quarrels. He was universally detested and also feared. Every one in the camp desired to see him humbled.

One day Shunan was particularly offensive. That morning he had engaged in two fights, and had knocked down and flogged both of the men whom he had assailed. The traders had brought whiskey to the rendezvous, and probably whiskey was at the bottom of these troubles. Mr. Carson was quietly talking with some of his friends, in one part of the extended encampment, when the swaggering bully came along seeking to provoke another fight. "These Americans," said he, "are all cowards; they are all women. I am going into the bush to cut some rods and I'll switch every one of them."

Kit Carson immediately stepped forward in his

calm, unimpassioned way, and with his soft and almost feminine voice said:

"Captain Shunan, I am an American and one of the smallest and weakest of them all. We have no disposition to quarrel with any one. But this conduct can no longer be endured. If it is continued, I shall be under the necessity of shooting you."

There was almost a magic power in Kit Carson's calmness. He had a piercing eye, before whose glance many would quail. There was an indescribable something in his soft words, which indicated that they came from a lion-like heart. The whole company of trappers looked on in perfect silence, curious to see what would be the result of this bold movement.

Shunan at first, the herculean bully, looked down upon his fragile opponent, with much of the contempt with which Goliath contemplated David. But apparently that glance showed him that he had encountered no ordinary foe. The reputation also of Kit Carson, as an able and fearless man extended through the whole encampment. There was a moment of perfect silence, Shunan not uttering one word in reply. He then turned upon his heel and walked rapidly across the plain towards his camp. Carson and the mountaineers understood perfectly what this meant. He had gone to seize his rifle, mount his horse, and shoot Kit Carson for defying him.

Carson also turned his steps towards his own lodge. He took a loaded pistol, bestrode his horse, and saw Shunan riding down towards him rifle in hand. All this had occupied but a few minutes. Still it had arrested the attention of nearly the whole encampment. It was well known that when Carson and Shunan should meet on the hostile field, there was to be no vulgar rough and tussle fight, but a decisive conflict which would settle forever the question, whether the one or the other was to be master. The common law of the wilderness demanded only, that the parties should be left to settle the question in their own way.

Kit Carson always rode a magnificent horse. He bestrode his steed as if he were a part of the animal, and seemed as unembarrassed in his movements when in the saddle, as when on the floor of his tent. Rapidly he rode down upon Shunan until the heads of their horses nearly touched. Calmly he inquired, as if it were one of the most ordinary occurrences of life.

"Am I the person you are looking for?" The treacherous bully answered. "No," hoping thus, in some degree, to throw his opponent off his guard; but at the same instant, he brought his rifle to his shoulder with the muzzle not four feet from the heart of his intended victim. The life of Carson depended upon the fraction of a moment. We call him a lucky man; we should rather say, he was a wise man prepared for every emergency. His pistol was in his hand, cocked and primed. Quick as a flash, it was raised, not at the heart, but at the right arm of the insolent bully, whom he would bring to order.

So simultaneous was the discharge of both weapons, that but one report was heard. But Carson's bullet entered upon its mission probably half a second before the ball of Shunan left the rifle. Shunan's wrist was shattered, as the bullet struck it; and from the curvature of the arm the ball passed through a second time above the elbow. The sudden shock caused the rifle to tilt a little upwards and thus saved the hero's life. Carson's face was severely burned by the powder, and the ball glanced over the top of his head, just cutting through the skin. The bully's rifle dropped from his hand. He had received a terrible and an utterly disabling wound. He had fought his last battle. No surgery could ever heal those fractured bones so as to put that arm again in fighting trim. The wretch had sought the life of Carson; but Carson had sought only to subdue the tyrant.

Shunan was thoroughly humbled, and became as

docile as a child. They took him to his tent, and treated him with all the rough nursing which trappers in the wilderness could bestow. The shattered bones of course could never recover their former strength. The weakest of those upon whom he formerly trampled, could now chastise him, should he assume any of his former insolent airs. The tyrant became docile as a child, and the whole camp regarded Carson as its benefactor.

It is worthy of special notice, that Mr. Carson was not at all elated by his victory. He never boasted of it. He never alluded to it, but with a saddened countenance. Whenever the subject was referred to, he always expressed his heartfelt regret, that it had been needful to resort to such severe measures to preserve the good order of the camp.

In the life of John Charles Fremont we find the following reference to Mr. Carson and to this adventure:

"Christopher Carson is a remarkably peaceable and quiet man, temperate in his habits, and strictly moral in his deportment." In a letter written from California in 1847, introducing Carson as the bearer of dispatches to the government, Col. Fremont says:

"'With me Carson and Truth, mean the same thing. He is always the same,—gallant and disinterested.'

"He is kind-hearted and averse to all quarrelsome and turbulent scenes, and has never been engaged in any mere personal broils or encounters, except on one single occasion, which he sometimes modestly describes to his friends. The narrative is fully confirmed by an eye-witness, of whose presence at the time he was not aware, and whose account he has probably never seen."

Another who knew him well, writes, in corroborative testimony:

"The name of Christopher Carson has been familarly known for nearly a quarter of a century. From its association with the names of great explorers and military men, it is now spread throughout the civilized world. It has been generally conceded, that no small share of the benefits derived from these explorations, was due to the sagacity, skill, experience, advice and labor of Christopher Carson. His sober habits, strict honor, and great regard for truth, have endeared him to all who can call him friend; and among such may be enumerated, names belonging to some of the most distinguished men whose deeds are recorded on the pages of American history.

"A few years ago, the writer of this first met Christopher Carson. It needed neither a second introduction, nor the assistance of a friendly panegyric, to enable him to discover, in Christopher Carson, those traits of manhood which are esteemed by the great and good to be the distinguishing ornaments of character. This acquaintance ripened into a friendship of the purest stamp. Since then the writer has been the intimate friend and companion of Christopher Carson at his home, in the wild scenes of the chase, on the war trail, and upon the field of battle.

"Christopher Carson physically, is small in stature, but of compact framework. He has a large and finely developed head, a twinkling grey eye, and hair of a sandy color which he wears combed back. His education having been much neglected in his youth, he is deficient in theoretical learning. By natural abilities, however, he has greatly compensated for this defect. He speaks the French and Spanish languages fluently, besides being a perfect master of several Indian dialects. In Indian customs, their manners, habits, and the groundwork of their conduct, no man on the American Continent is better skilled."

## CHAPTER VII.

### *War with the Blackfeet Indians.*

Unsuccessful Trapping.—Disastrous March to Fort Hall.—The Feast upon Horse-flesh.—The Hunting Expedition.—Its Rare Attractions.—Dogged by the Blackfeet.—Safe Arrival at the Fort.—All their Animals Stolen by the Indians.—Expedition to the Blackfeet Country.—Winter Quarters with the Friendly Indians.—Sufferings of the Animals.—Return to the Blackfeet Country.—Battle with the Indians.—Incidents of the Battle.

AT the close of the summer months the rendezvous was broken up, and all parties scattered; the traders to their homes, within the precincts of civilization, and the trappers to the savage wilderness. Kit Carson joined a party bound to the upper waters of the Yellowstone river. This is a large stream with many tributaries, all of which take their rise amidst the eastern ravines of the Rocky mountains, pouring their united flood into the Missouri at Fort William. From the head waters of the river, to the point where it enters the Missouri, there is a distance of five or six hundred miles, of perhaps as wild a country as can be found on this continent.

Here, amidst these rugged defiles, the mountaineers set their traps. But they caught no beaver. They then struck across the country, in a southeast direction, a distance of one or two hundred miles, to the Big Horn river, another large tributary of the Yellowstone. Here again they were unsuccessful. They then journeyed westward, several hundred miles, to what are called the Three Forks of the Missouri river. Here again they set their traps in vain. Our disappointed but persistent trappers turned their footsteps south, and having travelled about two hundred miles, passing through one of the defiles of the Rocky mountains, they reached the head waters of the Big Snake river. This is a large stream, some six hundred miles in length, which pours its flood through the Columbia river into the Pacific Ocean.

Here Kit Carson met a Mr. McCoy, formerly a trader in the employment of the Hudson Bay Company, but who was now out on a trapping excursion. With the consent of his companions, Kit Carson and five others withdrew from the larger party to join their fortunes with Mr. McCoy. A rumor had reached them that abundance of beaver were to be found at a distance of about one hundred and fifty miles, on Mary's river, since called the Humboldt. Here again they were doomed to disappointment. They followed down this stream, trapping in vain, for a hundred miles, till its waters were lost in what is called the Great Basin.

These hardy adventurers now directed their steps north, and after traversing a country, most of it wild and barren, about two hundred miles in extent, again reached the banks of the Snake river, midway between its source and its mouth. Here the company divided. Mr. McCoy set out to trap down the stream, about one hundred and fifty miles, to Fort Walla Walla, which was near the junction of this river with the Columbia.

Kit Carson and his band followed up the stream about the same distance, trapping most of the way. They, however, encountered continued disappointments. The region they traversed was dreary and barren in the extreme. Often there was no game to be found. They were brought to the very verge of starvation. For some time they subsisted upon nutritious roots, which they had adopted the precaution to take with them. When these were exhausted they were reduced to the greatest straits, and could be only saved from starving by bleeding the mules and drinking the warm blood. This is a resource which could not be repeated. The animals were also very poor, though enough of dry and scanty grass was found to keep them alive.

The whole party became frightfully emaciated,

and they began to fear that they should be compelled to kill some of their mules. But the men themselves had become so weak it was with difficulty they could carry their rifles. The loss of any of these useful beasts of burden would terribly enhance their peril. It might compel them to abandon, not only their traps, but also their rifles and their ammunition. In this dreadful emergency they came across a band of Indians who proved to be friendly. But the savages were also in an extremely destitute condition.

Fortunately for both parties there was water at hand, and the withered herbage furnished the animals with sustenance. The Indians had a young horse which was respectably fat. It required all of Kit Carson's diplomatic skill and knowledge of the Indian character to induce the Indians to part with the animal. It was not until after much maneuvering that they succeeded in obtaining him. He was immediately killed and eaten. To the hungry men, the horse flesh afforded as delicious a feast as epicure ever found in the most costly viands.

At last Kit Carson and his men reached Fort Hall. Here they were, of course, kindly received by their countrymen, and all their wants were immediately and abundantly supplied. This fort was then mainly occupied as a trading post. As the men were neither sick nor wounded, but only half starved, they found themselves in a few days quite recruited, and ready again for any adventure of enterprise and hard ship. During their sojourn at the fort the men were not idle. They had their saddles, clothing and moccasins to repair. All their outfit was in the condition of a ship which has just weathered a storm with loss of anchor, sails, spars, and leaking badly.

Having finished their repairs the party, in good condition, with their mules, set out on a hunting expedition. They were told that in a fertile region, about fifty miles south of them, large herds of buffaloes had recently been seen. The weather was delightful. They were all in good spirits. It was trapper philosophy never to anticipate evil,—never to borrow any trouble. At a rapid pace they marched through a pleasant, luxuriant well watered region, entirely forgetful of past sufferings.

On the evening of the second day, as they were emerging from a forest, there was opened before them a scene of remarkable beauty and grandeur. Far as the eye could extend towards the south, east and west an undulating prairie spread, with its wilderness of flowers of every gorgeous hue, waving in the evening breeze like the gently heaving ocean. The sun was just setting in a cloudless sky, illuminating with extraordinary brilliance the enchanting scene. Here and there in the distance of the boundless plain, a few clumps of trees were scattered, as if nature had arranged them with the special purpose of decorating the Eden-like landscape. But that which cheered the hunters more than all the other aspects of sublimity and loveliness, were the immense herds, grazing on the apparently limitless prairie. Many of these herds numbered thousands and yet they appeared but like little spots scattered over the vast expanse. The hunter had found his paradise; for there were other varieties of game in that luxuriant pasture, elk, deer, antelopes and there was room enough for them all.

Our adventurers immediately selected a spot for their camp on the edge of the forest, near a bubbling spring. With great alacrity they reared their hut, and arranged all the apparatus for camping, with which they were abundantly supplied. Poles were cut from the forest, and planted in the open sunny prairie, with ropes of hide stretched upon them. Upon these ropes they were to suspend strips of buffalo meat to be cured by drying in the sun. Every thing was prepared over night for the commencement of operations in the early dawn. The best marksmen were selected for hunters. They were to go into the prairie, shoot the game and bring it in. The rest were detailed to cut up the meat and hang it on the ropes to dry. After it was sufficiently dried, they were to take it down, and pack it closely in bundles for transportation.

These were halcyon days, and abundant was the harvest of game which these bold reapers were gathering. During the days thus spent, in shooting the game and curing the meat, the hunters lived upon the fat of the land. The tongue and liver of the buffalo, and the peculiar fat, found along the spine are deemed great delicacies.

In a few days a sufficient supply had been obtained to load all their pack animals. So heavily were they laden that their homeward journey was very slow. They were followed by a foe, of whom they had not the slightest conception. A band of Blackfeet Indians had discerned them from the far distance with their keen eyes. Keeping carefully concealed, they watched every movement of the unconscious hunters. When the party commenced its return they dogged their steps; in the darkness creeping near their encampment at night, watching for an opportunity to stampede their animals and to rob them of their treasure. Though Kit Carson had no suspicion that any savages were on his trail, his constitutional caution baffled all their cunning.

The fort was reached in safety, and the abundance which they brought was hailed with rejoicing. The party of hunters encamped just outside the pickets of the fort, where there was good pasturage for their animals, and where they could watch them. The inmates of the fort had fenced in a large field or barnyard which they called a *corral.* Into this yard at night they drove their animals, from the prairie, and placed a guard over them. At any time a band of savages might, like an apparition, come shrieking down upon the animals to bear them away in the terrors of a stampede, or might silently, in midnight gloom, steal towards them and lead them noiselessly away one by one.

Two or three nights after the arrival of the hunters at the fort, all the horses and mules were driven, as usual, into the enclosure; the bars were put up and a sentinel was placed on duty. It so happened that the sentinel, that night, was an inexperienced hand; a new comer, not familiar with the customs of the fort. He was stationed, at a slight distance from the enclosure, where he could watch all its approaches, and give the alarm should any band of Indians appear. He supposed that a large, well mounted band alone would attempt the hazardous enterprise of capturing the animals.

The latter part of the night, just before the dawn of the morning, he saw two men advance, without any disguise, deliberately let down the bars and drive out the horses and mules. He supposed them to be two of the inmates of the fort or some of his own companions, who were authorized to take out the herd to graze upon the prairie. Concluding therefore that he was relieved from duty, he returned to his camp and was soon fast asleep.

In the morning the horses and mules had all disappeared. They were nowhere to be seen. There was hurrying to and fro, for a solution of the mystery, when a short investigation revealed the true state of affairs. The cunning Indians had come in a strong party, well mounted, and were concealed at a short distance. Two of their number had gone forward and driven out the animals. The horses and mules are always ready to rush along with any herd leading them.

Placing the stolen animals between the van and the rear guards of their steeds, the Indians moved cautiously until they had gained some little distance from the fort. Then giving the rein to their powerful charges, with the fleetness of the wind they fled, over the hills and through the valleys, to their wild and distant fastnesses.

Not a single animal was left for the garrison or the trappers upon which to give chase. The Indians, who have but little sense of right and wrong, might well exult in their achievement. Without the loss of a single man, and even without receiving a wound, they had taken from beneath the very walls of the fort, its whole herd, leaving the garrison powerless to pursue. The loss was very severe to the trappers. Without their horses and mules, they could do nothing. It only remained for them to wait for the return of Mr. McCoy and his party, who had promised, after visiting Fort Walla Walla, to rendezvous at Fort Hall.

The Blackfeet Indians were at that time, forty years ago, the terror of the whole region. It is said that the warlike tribe numbered thirty thousand souls. Of course there could not have been any very accurate estimate of the population, Not long after this the small-pox prevailed, with awful fatality. One half of the tribe perished. The dead were left unburied, as the savages endeavored to flee in all directions from the fearful pestilence.

A month passed slowly away before Mr. McCoy with his party reached the fort. Very opportunely he brought a fresh supply of animals; having purchased a number at Fort Walla Walla. The united band returned to the Green river. Here Mr. Carson joined a party of one hundred trappers who, in their strength, were to plunge into the very heart of the Blackfeet country, on the Yellowstone river.

Arriving at the region where they were to set

their traps, they divided into two companies of fifty men each. It was necessary to be always armed and on the alert, ready to repel any sudden attack. The duty of one company was to explore the streams in search of beavers and game for food. The other party guarded the camp, dressed, rudely tanned, and packed the skins, and cooked the food. The trappers were so strong, that they not only went where they pleased, but they were eager to come in contact with the savages, that they might pay off old scores. They were, however, not molested. Not an Indian crossed their path. They subsequently learned, as a solution of the mystery, that at that time the small-pox was making dreadful ravages. Thousands were dying and it was feared the whole tribe would perish. The Indians in their terror, had secluded themselves in the remotest solitudes.

Winter was now approaching, with its freezing gales, its drifting snows, its icy streams. It was necessary to find winter quarters for two or three months. The region, drained by the Yellowstone and its tributaries, extends over thousands of square miles. In one portion of the territory there was a mountainous region inhabited by the Crow Indians. As they were the deadly foe of the Blackfeet tribe, they were disposed to cultivate friendly relations with the whites, and to enter into an alliance with them.

Quite a large band of the Crow Indians joined the trappers, and conducted them to one of their most sheltered valleys. Here they reared their huts and lodges. The mountain ridges broke the force of the cold north wind. They had water and fuel in abundance. Game was not scarce and they had also an ample supply of dried meat in store. But as the season advanced, the cold became increasingly severe, until at last it was more intense than the trappers had ever before experienced. Still the trappers, with their rousing fires and abundant clothing, found no difficulty in keeping warm.

But the animals suffered terribly. Snow covered the valleys to such a depth, that they could obtain no food by grazing. It was with the utmost difficulty they kept the animals alive. They cut down cotton-wood trees and thawed the bark and small branches by their fires. This bark was then torn into shreds, sufficiently small for the animal to chew. The rough outside bark was thrown aside, and the tender inner bark, which comes next the body of the tree, was carefully peeled off for food. There is sufficient nutrition in this barely to keep the animals alive for a time, but they can by no means thrive under it.

Quite a company of Indians reared their lodges in the same valley with the trappers. In the pleasant days they vied with each other, in various athletic games, and particularly in their skill in hunting. Both parties were very happy in this truly paternal intercourse. There were no quarrels, for there was no whiskey there. One barrel of intoxicating drink would have changed kindly greetings into hateful brawls, and would have crimsoned many knives. Independently of the anxiety, the trappers felt for their suffering animals, the six or eight weeks of wintry cold passed away very pleasantly. The returning sun of spring poured its warmth into the sheltered valley, melting the snows and releasing the streams. With wonderful rapidity the swelling bud gave place to leaves and blossoms. The green grass sprang up on the mounds, the animals rejoiced and began even to prance in their new-found vigor. The winter had gone and the time for the singing of birds had come.

The trappers were in need of certain supplies, before they could advantageously set out on their spring hunting tour. They therefore sent two of their party to obtain these supplies at Fort Laramie, which was one or two hundred miles south of them, on the Platte river. They did not return. They were never heard from. It is probable that they fell into the hands of hostile Indians, who killed them and took possession of all their effects. This was another of those innumerable tragedies, ever occurring in this wicked world, which are only recorded in God's book of remembrance.

The trappers, after waiting for their companions for some time, were compelled to enter upon their spring hunt without them. They continued for some time setting their traps on the Yellowstone river, and then struck over to what is called the Twenty five yard river. After spending a few weeks there, they pushed on to the upper waters of the Missouri, where those waters flow through the most rugged ravines of the Rocky mountains. Here again they were in the vicinity of their Blackfeet foes. And they learned, through some wanderer in the wilderness, that the main village of that tribe was at the distance of but a few miles from them.

In the previous collisions between the Blackfeet and the trappers, the Indians had gained decidedly the advantage. They had at one time driven the trappers entirely out of their country, having stolen their traps, and effectually prevented them from taking furs. In the conflict, in which Kit Carson was wounded, the Indians had retired, though with loss, still victorious, carrying with them all their booty of stolen horses. Most humiliating of all, they had, without firing a shot, captured all the animals of the garrison and the trappers at Fort Hall. And it was most probable that they had robbed and murdered the two men who had been sent to fort Laramie.

The trappers were all burning to avenge these wrongs. The thievish Blackfeet had made these assaults upon them entirely unprovoked. The savages were greatly elated with their victories, and it was deemed essential that they should be so thoroughly chastised, that they would no longer molest those who were hunting and trapping within those wild solitudes. The whole party of trappers struck the trail which led to the Indian encampment, and cautiously followed it, until they were within ten or fifteen miles of their foes.

The company, numbering a hundred men, with one or two hundred horses and mules, presented a very imposing cavalcade. A council of war was held, and Kit Carson, with five picked men was sent forward to reconnoitre the position of the village, and to decide upon the best points of attack. The rest of the company retired to some little distance from the trail, where they concealed themselves, obliterating, as far as possible, their tracks. It was deemed necessary to proceed with the utmost caution. The Blackfeet composed one of the most numerous and ferocious of all the Indian tribes. Their warriors were numbered by thousands. It was certain that they would fight, and that a high degree of intelligence would guide them in the battle.

After the lapse of a few hours, Kit Carson returned from his perilous adventure. He had attained an eminence from which he could look down upon the valleys of the foe, which was in one part of an extended plain in the midst of hills. He reported that there was some great agitation in the camp. There were runnings to and fro, driving in the animals from their pasturage, saddling and packing them, and sundry other preparations indicative of a general alarm. It might be that their braves were entering on the war-path. It might be that they were preparing for flight. It was not improbable that, through their scouts, they had gained intimation of the approach of the trappers. A council of war was held. Promptly it was decided to send out forty-three men, under the leadership of Kit Carson to give the Blackfeet battle. The remaining men, fifty-five in number, were left, under Mr. Fontenelle, to discharge the responsible duty of guarding the animals and the equipage. They were also to move slowly on, as a reserve force, who could rush to the aid of the advanced force, or upon which those men could fall back in case of disaster.

They soon reached the village. It was pretty evident that they were expected. But the savages had only bows and arrows. This gave the assailants an immense advantage. They had both rifles and pistols. Taking a circuitous route, they approached the village from an unexpected quarter. They were scarcely seen before a discharge of their guns struck down ten of the bravest warriors. But at that time it was an encampment rather than a village, occupied mainly by fighting men, who greatly outnumbered their assailants. The Indians fought heroically. Each man instantly sprang behind some tree where, protected, he could watch his opportunity and keep his foe at a distance. When a rifle was once discharged, it took some time to reload; but the Indians could throw a dozen arrows in a minute, with sinewy arms, with sure aim and with deadly power.

The battle was mainly in the forest, neither party being willing to encountre the exposure of the open plain. The Indians, behind the trees, watched their opportunity. As there were several Indians to one white man, and the trappers were necessarily dispersed, seeking the protection of the trees, the Indians, as soon as a rifle was discharged, would dodge from tree to tree, ever drawing nearer to their assailants. For three hours this battle continued. The ammunition of the trappers was nearly exhausted, and they remitted the energy of their fire, awaiting the arrival of their companions. The Indians comprehended the state of things and sagaciously resolved to make a simultaneous charge, before the trappers should have opportunity to replenish their powder-horns and bullet-pouches.

There was a distance of many rods between the two contending parties. The ground was mainly level, and there was no underbrush to intercept the view. The trappers saw and understood the movement for the charge. Every man was prepared, with his loaded rifle and revolver. On came the Indians, dodging, as they could, from tree to tree, but with an impetuosity of onset which excited the admiration of their opponents. The forest resounded with their shrill war-whoop. Carson requested every man to withhold his fire until sure of his aim. "Let not a single shot," said he, "be lost." It was a fearful moment, for upon that moment depended the life of every man in the party. Should the outnumbering Indians succeed in passing the narrow intervening space, the trappers would inevitably be overpowered and from the spear-heads of the savages, forty-three scalps would be waved as the banners of their victory.

There was no simultaneous discharge but a rattling fire, occupying perhaps sixty seconds. Forty-three Indian warriors were struck by the bullets. Eleven fell instantly dead; the others were more or less crippled by their wounds. Still the brave Indians rushed on, when suddenly there was opened upon them another deadly fire from the revolvers. This was a reinforcement of the strength of their foes which the savages had not anticipated. They hesitated, staggered as if smitten by a heavy blow, and then slowly and sullenly retreated, until they were far beyond pistol range. Some of the mountaineers were on horseback to carry swift aid to any imperilled comrade. Kit Carson was also mounted and with his eagle eye was watching every act of his little army.

One of his aids, a mountaineer by the name of Cotton, was thrown from his horse, which slipped upon some smooth stones, and fell upon his rider, fastening him helpless to the ground. Six Indians near by rushed, with exultant yells and gleaming tomahawks, for his scalp. Kit Carson, calling on two or three to follow him, sprang from his horse and with the speed of an antelope was by the side of his fallen comrade. The crack of his rifle was instantly heard; the foremost of the savages gave one convulsive bound, uttered a death cry and fell weltering in his blood. The rest immediately fled, but before they could reach a place of safety three more were struck down by the balls of those who had followed Carson. Two only of the six savages escaped.

# CHAPTER VIII

## *Encampments and Battles.*

**The** Renewal of the Battle.—Peculiarities of the Fight.—**The Rout.** —Encampment in the Indian Village.—Number of Trappers among the Mountains.—The New Rendezvous.—Picturesque Scene of the Encampment.—The Missionary and the Nobleman. —Brown's Hole.—The Navajoes.—Kit Carson Purveyor at the Fort.—Trapping at the Black Hills.—Again upon the Yellowstone.—Pleasant Winter Quarters.—Signs of the Indians.—Severe Conflict.—Reappearance of the Indians.—Their utter Discomfiture.

THERE was now a brief lull in the battle. The Indians had not left the field and by no means acknowledged a defeat. With very considerable military skill they selected a new position for the renewal of the fight, on broken ground among a chaos of rocks, about one hundred and fifty yards from the line of their opponents. They were evidently aware of the strong reserve approaching to join the trappers. With this reserve it was necessary that the trappers should make the attack, for they could not venture to move on their way leaving so powerful a hostile army behind them.

The Indians manifested very considerable powers

of reasoning, and no little strategic skill. They took the defensive, and chose a position from which it would be almost impossible to dislodge them. The trappers awaited the arrival of their comrades, and obtained a fresh supply of ammunition. The whole united band prepared for a renewal of the battle. Thus far not one of the trappers had been wounded, excepting Cotton, who was severely bruised by the fall of his horse.

About an half hour elapsed while these movements were taking place with each party. The trappers all dismounted and then, in a long line, with cheers advanced in Indian fashion, from tree to tree, from rock to rock, every moment drawing nearer to their determined foes. The great battle, the Waterloo conflict, now commenced. Small as were the numbers engaged, limited as was the field of action, there was perhaps never a battle in which more personal courage was displayed, or in which more skill and endurance was called into requisition. Not unfrequently a trapper would occupy one side of a large boulder and an Indian warrior the other, each watching for the life of his adversary, while every fibre of mental and muscular power were roused to activity. Neither could leave his covert without certain death, and one or the other must inevitably fall.

For an hour or two this dreadful conflict continued. Gradually the superiority of the white man, and the vast advantage which the rifle gave, began to be manifest. The Indians were slowly driven back, from tree to rock, from rock to tree. Many of their warriors had fallen in death. The ground was crimsoned with their blood. The disheartened Indians began to waver, then to retreat; and then as the trappers made a simultaneous charge, and the rifle bullets whistled around them, to run in complete rout, scattering in all directions. It was in vain to attempt any pursuit. The women and children of the Blackfeet village were on an eminence, about a mile from their homes, awaiting the issue of the conflict. They also instantly disappeared, seeking refuge no one knew where.

In this battle a large number of the Indians were killed or wounded, we know not how many. But three of the trappers were killed, though many others received wounds more or less severe. The Indian village was located on very fine camping-ground. They left nothing behind them. An Indian woman needs no Saratoga trunk for her wardrobe. Their comfortable wigwams were left standing. Here Fontenelle allowed his party to rest for several days. The dead were to be buried, the wounded to be nursed, damages to be repaired, and a new supply of provisions to be obtained. Free from all fear of molestation, the trappers explored the region for miles around, and were very successful in taking beavers.

It is estimated that the various parties of trappers, then wandering among the mountains, numbered at least six hundred men. While our trappers were thus encamped, elated with their victory over the Indians, and still more exultant over their daily success in trapping and hunting, one day an express rode into the camp, and informed them that the rendezvous was to be held, that year, upon the Mud river, a small stream flowing circuitously from the south into Green river. The party, having a large stock of beaver on hand, set out to cross the main ridge of the Rocky mountains, to dispose of their furs at the rendezvous. It required a journey of eight days. As the trapping party, nearly a hundred in number, all mounted on gayly caparisoned steeds, and leading one or two hundred pack horses, entered the valley over the distant eminences, there were two scenes presented to the eye, each peculiar in many aspects of sublimity and beauty.

It was midsummer. The smooth meadow upon which the encampment was held was rich, verdant and blooming, a beautiful stream flowing along its western border. A fine grove fringed the stream as far as the eye could reach up and down. Not a tree, stump, or stone was to be seen upon the smooth, lawn-like expanse. Its edge, near the grove, was lined with a great variety of lodges, constructed of skins or bark, or of forest boughs. Horses and mules in great numbers were feeding on the rich herbage, while groups of trappers, Canadians, Frenchmen, Americans and Indians, were scattered around, some cooking at their fires, some engaged in eager traffic, and some amusing themselves in athletic sports. It was a peaceful scene, where, so far as the eye could discern, man's fraternity was combined with nature's loveliness to make this a happy world. Such was the spectacle presented to the trappers as they descended into the valley.

On the other hand, the trappers themselves contributed a very important addition to the picturesqueness of the view. Half a mile from the encampment, in the northeast, the land rose in a gentle, gradual swell, smooth, verdant and treeless, perhaps to the height of a hundred and fifty feet. Down this declivity they were descending, with their horses and their pack mules, in a long line of single file. They were way-worn pilgrims, and the grotesqueness of their attire, and their unshaven, uncut, and almost uncombed locks, added to their weird-like aspect.

Here the party met with two gentlemen, such as were rarely, perhaps never before, seen on such an occasion. One was a Christian missionary, Father De Smidt, who, in obedience to the Saviour's commission, "Go ye into all the world and preach my Gospel to every creature," had abandoned the comforts of civilization, to cast in his lot with the savages, that he might teach them that religion of the Bible which would redeem the world by leading all men to repentance, to faith in an atoning Saviour, and to endeavor "to do justly, to love mercy, and to walk humbly with God."

The other stranger was an English nobleman, a gentleman of high character, of refinement and culture. In his ancestral home he had heard of the sublimities of the wilderness; the wide-spread prairies; the gloomy forests; the solitary lakes. He had heard of savage men, numbering tens of thousands in their tribes, almost as wild, as devoid of human traits as were the buffaloes whom they pursued with whoop and halloo over the plains. Curiosity, a very rational and praiseworthy curiosity, had lured him into these remote realms, that he might behold the wondrous works of God, and that he might study the condition of his brother man without the Gospel.

Kit Carson was, by a natural instinct, drawn into

association with this refined English gentleman. They could each appreciate the other. They soon became acquainted, and a warm friendship sprang up between them. Mr. Carson subsequently wrote, in reference to Sir William Stuart:

"For the goodness of his heart and numerous rare qualities of his mind, he will always be remembered by those of the mountaineers who had the honor of his acquaintance."

The terms of the commendation show the virtues which Mr. Carson could appreciate, and which he was accustomed to practice. Of the missionary, Rev. Mr. De Smidt, it has been very truly written:

"Perhaps there never was a person, in the wilds of America, who became so universally beloved, both by the white and red man. While in the mountains he acted with untiring zeal for the good of all with whom he came into contact. Wherever duty called him, there he was sure to be found, no matter what the obstacles or dangers spread upon his path. He worked during a long series of years in these dangerous localities, and when he at length returned to civilization he left an indelible name behind him."

The Rendezvous continued for twenty days. It was a constant festival, like the Olympic games of the Greeks, or the renowned Tournaments of more modern days, with the exception that business was intimately blended with pleasures. It at length broke up into small parties. Kit Carson, with seven companions, followed down the Green river, to Brown's Hole; a narrow but sunny and fertile valley about sixteen miles long. Here he found a party of traders, who were on an excursion to a numerous and quite wealthy band of Indians, called the Navajoes. They seemed to have attained a degree of civilization considerably above that of any of the other tribes. They had fixed abodes; had immense herds of sheep, horses and mules. They had also attained, the art by a slow and tedious process, of weaving admirable woolen blankets; thick, warm and strong. These blankets were quite renowned throughout all that region, and brought a high price. Kit Carson joined the traders in their expedition to the country of the Navajoes.

Here they purchased many of these blankets, and a large drove of strong, fat mules. With these they crossed the mountains, to a distance of three or four hundred miles, to a fort on the south fork of the Platte river. At this place they disposed of their blankets and cattle to great advantage, and Mr. Carson promptly returned to the companions he had left at Brown's Hole. The traders undoubtedly received in payment the only currency of the country, beaver skins. These they probably took with them to St. Louis for ultimate sale. We know not how Mr. Carson invested his earnings. It is very certain that he did not squander them in riotous living. Subsequent events indicate that they were sent through the hands of the traders, Messrs. Thompson and Sinclair, to the States, there to be deposited to his credit.

The autumnal months had now passed away, and the blasts of approaching winter warned the hunters that they must seek a refuge from its storms.

Mr. Carson had produced so favorable an impression upon the men at the fort on the Platte river, that they sent him a very urgent invitation to return, and take the very responsible position of steward or purveyor for the garrison during the winter. They offered him such ample emolument that he accepted their proposition, though many other parties were eager to obtain his services. I cannot help remarking, in this connection, in special reference to any of my young readers, that this is the true secret of success in life. In whatever position you are, in whatever business you are engaged, be as faithful and perfect as possible. Promotion and prosperity are then almost sure.

The task which now devolved upon Mr. Carson was, with his rifle and such aid as he might need, to supply all the animal food which twenty men might require. He performed this duty, not only to the satisfaction of all, but such was his energy, his skill, his spirit of self-sacrifice, his entire devotion to his work, and the wonderful success which attended his exertions, that he secured universal affection and esteem.

With the returning sun of spring, Mr. Carson, having well performed his task, joined Mr. Bridger and four other trappers, to go to what were called the Black Hills. This was a limited mountainous range, far away in the north, extending a distance of about a hundred miles between the Laramie and Sweetwater rivers. These streams were tributaries of the north fork of the Platte. This region had perhaps never before been visited by either trapper or hunter. They found beavers in plenty, and their success was excellent.

With well laden mules they again crossed the Rocky mountains to reunite themselves with the main camp of the trappers on Green river. They trapped on their way and continued success attended them. Thus enriched, they accompanied the main party to a tributary of the Wind river, where the annual Rendezvous was that year to be held. Here were renewed the usual scenes of the trapper's great Fair which we have already described.

As the Rendezvous broke up, Mr. Carson joined

a large party, and recrossed the mountains to the Yellowstone, where they had already had so many bloody encounters with the Blackfeet Indians. They trapped successfully until the inclement weather forced them into winter quarters. Nothing occurred of any moment, until mid-winter. Daily parties went out for game and they always returned with an ample supply. In their snug lodges, gathered around their blazing fires, telling stories of past adventures, preparing clothing for the summer, feasting upon fat turkeys, and the choicest cuts of buffalo-meat and venison, a few weeks passed very pleasantly away. Being free from that most terrible of all earthly curses, intoxicating drinks, there was no discord, and this little community of mountaineers, in the solitudes of a Rocky mountain valley, were perhaps as happy as any other equal community amidst the highest conveniences of civilization.

One winter's day a little band of hunters, in their pursuit of game, were lured to a greater distance than usual from the camp. Their attention was arrested by certain signs which indicated that a band of Indians had passed by, and had endeavored carefully to conceal their trail. A close scrutiny so confirmed this opinion that they hastily returned to the camp with the declaration that savages were certainly prowling around watching for an opportunity to attack them. They knew full well that the wary Indians would never think of approaching their camp unless in overpowering numbers. It was deemed expedient not to allow the foe any time to mature their plans. A party of forty men was immediately fitted out, under the command of Kit Carson, to go to the hidden trail and follow it till the haunts of the Indians were discovered. The reputation of Mr. Carson was such that unanimously he was invested with dictatorial powers. Everything was left to the decision of his own good judgment.

With silent, moccasined tread the adventurers threaded their way over the broken country, and through a dense forest, when suddenly they came upon a band of Indians, manifestly on the war-path; painted, plumed and armed in the highest style of their barbaric art. The savages, on catching sight of the trappers, turned and fled with the utmost speed, without scattering. The trappers pursued with equal swiftness of foot. They had no doubt that there was a stronger band at some little distance, which the Indians were retreating to join.

The supposition proved correct. A large number of warriors had assembled, in a very good military position, and it was at once evident that they intended to give battle. Though the majority of them had only arrows and lances, many were armed with rifles.

They were on a hill-side which was quite steep, rugged with boulders, and with a heavy growth of gloomy firs and pines. The field was admirably adapted for the Indian mode of warfare, and the desperate warriors of the Blackfeet were foes not to be despised.

Kit Carson possessed the qualities essential to a military leader. He was cautious as he was bold. He was very careful never unnecessarily to expose the lives of his men. Very deliberately he reconnoitred the position, and prepared for the battle. He had no doubt that, with what would be called a gallant rush, he might drive the Indians from him and gain a brilliant victory. But it would be attended with loss. By a slower process he was sure of the result, while his men would be protected from death and wounds. All of his men were armed with the best of rifles. They had a good supply of ammunition. They could afford to load with heavy charges which would throw the balls to the greatest possible distance. It was very difficult for the Indians to obtain ammunition. They therefore found it necessary to husband the little they had with great care. Consequently the Indian's rifle, but lightly charged, would seldom throw a bullet more than two-thirds the distance thrown by the rifle of the trapper.

Mr. Carson gave every man his position. They were all veterans in every exigence of Indian warfare. Each man was capable of independent action. They all knew the folly of throwing away a single shot. There was no random firing. Each man was trained to seek sure protection behind rock, stump or tree, and then to keep a vigilant watch, not only to guard himself but his immediate comrades from the missiles of the foe. Slowly the line of trappers was to advance upon the enemy, from point to point of protection, making sure that every bullet should kill or wound. The tactics of the battle secured the victory. The Indians fought with their accustomed bravery. But one after another their warriors fell killed or disabled.

As the gloom of a winter's night settled down over this awful scene of war, the savages retired in good order, across the ice of an arm of the Yellowstone, to an island in the middle of the river. They had adopted the precaution, unusual with them, of erecting here quite a strong fortress, to which they could retreat in case of disaster. Thus situated, both parties, wearied with the long conflict of the day, sought such repose as night could give to men sleeping upon their arms.

The trappers knew not what scenes were transpiring in the Indian camp on the island. As for themselves, they could only venture, with the utmost caution, to kindle small fires to cook their supper.

They then carefully extinguished the embers, lest the flames should guide several hundred warriors in a midnight attack.

Mr. Carson was not aware of the strength of the Indian fortifications on the island. Not wishing to give them any time to strengthen their works, with the earliest dawn he put his men in motion. They crossed the ice to the island, where they found only silence and desolation. Not an Indian was to be seen. In the night the savages had retreated, and were then probably at a distance of leagues, no one could tell where. There were, however, many indications left of the results of the battle. The interior of the fort was quite crimsoned with fresh blood. A bloody trail led to a hole which they had cut through the ice in the middle of the river, and into which they had thrust the bodies of the slain. It was not their intention that the trappers should know how many of their number had been wounded or slain. Mr. Carson with his victorious associates returned to the camp.

A council of war was held. It was generally supposed that the powerful Blackfeet could bring five thousand warriors into the field. They were very resolute men; having been abundantly successful heretofore, it was not doubted they would strain every nerve to wipe out the disgrace of this defeat.

The trappers were confident that the savages would soon appear again, with numbers which they would deem sufficient to annihilate the white men. Guided by the wisdom of Kit Carson, the whole camp immediately resolved itself into a military garrison. Intrenchments were thrown up to guard every approach. Everything was cleared away, around the camp within rifle range, behind which an Indian could secrete himself. The most trusty men were appointed as sentinels.

About a mile from the camp there was an eminence, several hundred feet high, whose summit commanded a fine view of the whole surrounding country. Every day some one was sent to that hill to keep a constant lookout.

The wisdom of Mr. Carson's measures was soon apparent. One morning the watch on the hill discerned, far away in the distance, a warlike band of Indians approaching. He had no doubt that it was, as it proved to be, but the advanced guard of the Indian army. He waved his signal to communicate the intelligence to the camp, and immediately hastened down to join his comrades. Every man sprang to arms and was at his post. Kit Carson had anticipated everything and had attended to the most minute details.

With firm self-confident tread the savages came

on, a thousand in number, to crush by the weight of their onset, and to trample beneath their feet sixty trappers. It was an appalling sight even for brave men to look upon. They were all arrayed in their fantastic war costume, some on horseback splendidly mounted, some on foot, many armed with rifles, and others with bows, arrows, and lances which were very formidable weapons in the hands of such stalwart and sinewy men.

They came in separate bands, of two or three hundred each, and took position about a mile from the fort. As band after band came up, the prairie and the adjacent hills resounded with their yells of defiance. In the evening they held their war-dance, which the trappers well understood to be the sure precursor of the battle on the next day. Their songs could be distinctly heard in the camp, and as they danced, with hideous contortions, in the gathering shades of night around their fires, it seemed as though a band of demons had broken loose from Pandemonium.

With the first dawn of the morning, a large party of these warriors approached the fort to reconnoitre. They were evidently astonished in beholding the preparations which had been made to receive them. They could not, from any direction, approach within an eighth of a mile, without presenting their bodies a perfect target for the rifles of men who never missed their aim. These cautious warriors did not venture within half a mile of the fortress. But they were keen-eyed and sagacious men. They saw that the trappers were effectually protected by their breast-works, and that the fort could by no possibility be taken without enormous slaughter on their own side. Indeed it was doubtful whether, armed as the white men were, with rifles, revolvers and knives, the fort could be taken at any expense.

In their impotent rage a few random shots were fired at the fort, but the bullets did not reach their mark. The trappers threw away no lead. They quietly awaited the attack, and were so confident of their ability to defeat the Indians, that they were disappointed when they saw the reconnoitring party commencing to retire. They shouted to them in terms of derision, hoping to exasperate them into an attack. But the wary savages were not thus to be drawn to certain death. They retired to their camp, which as we have said was distant about a mile from the fort, but which was in perfect view.

Here they evidently held a general council of war. There probably was some diversity of opinion, as many speeches were made and the council was protracted for several hours. There was manifestly no enthusiasm on the occasion, and no exultant shouts were heard. At the conclusion of the council, the whole band divided into two parties and, in divergent directions, disappeared from view. After this the trappers were not again disturbed by the Indians. Indeed they feared no molestation. No Indian band would think of attacking a fortress which a thousand warriors had declared impregnable.

As soon as the returning spring would permit, the trappers broke up their encampment on the Yellowstone, and passing directly west through the very heart of the Blackfeet country, planted their traps on the head waters of the Missouri river. For three months they traversed many of the tributaries of this most majestic of streams. They were moderately successful, and in the early summer turned their steps south, crossing the mountains to dispose of their furs at the Rendezvous, which was again held on Green river. Here they remained in such social enjoyment as the great festival could afford them, until the month of August, when the Rendezvous was dissolved.

## CHAPTER IX.

### *The Trapper's Elysium.*

Trapping on the Missouri.—Attacked by the Blackfeet.—The Battle.—Persevering Hostility of the Indians.—The Trappers driven from the Country.—Repair to the North Fork.—Cheerful Encampments.—Enchanting Scene.—Village of the Flatheads.—The Blessings of Peace.—Carson's Knowledge of Languages.—Pleasant Winter Quarters on the Big Snake River.—Successful Trapping.—Winter at Brown's Hole.—Trip to Fort Bent.—Peculiar Characters.—Williams and Mitchel.—Hunter at Fort Bent.—Marriage.—Visit to the States.

UPON the breaking up of the rendezvous at Green river, Kit Carson, with five companions, directed his steps in a northwest course, about two hundred miles to Fort Hall, on Snake river. He spent the autumnal months trapping along the various streams in this region. They were very successful on this tour, and at the close of the season returned to the fort with a rich supply of furs. These forts were generally trading-houses, well fortified and garrisoned, but not governmental military posts.

Here Carson disposed of his furs to good advantage, and after remaining there about a month he crossed the mountains with a large party of trappers to the head waters of the Missouri, thus again entering the country of the Blackfeet. They struck the Missouri river itself far up among the mountains. They commenced setting their traps on this stream. Slowly they followed up the banks, gathering in the morning what they had taken through the night.

One morning a party of half a dozen trappers, who had gone about two miles from the camp to examine their traps, encountered a band of Blackfeet Indians, who fired upon them. The trappers immediately retreated with the greatest rapidity. Though closely pursued by their swift-footed foes they reached the camp in safety. It so happened that near their camp there was quite an extensive thicket of tall trees and dense underbrush. Kit Carson, not knowing how numerous the Indians might be who were coming upon him, directed the men as quickly as possible to conceal themselves and animals in the thicket.

Scarcely had the order been executed when the Indians with hideous yells came rushing towards the camp. But not a trapper or a horse was visible. Nothing was found there but silence and solitude. Still they came rushing on, shouting and brandishing their weapons, when suddenly and to their great consternation, the reports of the rifles were heard and fourteen bullets struck fourteen warriors. Several were killed outright, others were seriously wounded. Before the savages had recovered from their consternation the rifles were reloaded and every man was ready for another discharge.

The brave Blackfeet wavered for a moment, and then with unearthly yells, made a simultaneous charge upon the thicket. Carson was in the midst of his little band. His calm, soft voice was heard reassuring his men, as he said:

"Keep cool and fire as deliberately as if you were shooting at game."

There was another almost simultaneous discharge and every bullet struck a warrior. The Indians, thus mercilessly handled, recoiled, and every one sought refuge behind some trunk, rock or tree. They could see no foe, while the trappers could find peep-holes through which they could watch all the movements of the Indians. A shower of arrows was thrown into the thicket, but none of the trappers were struck. The intermittent battle continued the whole day. Several times the savages attempted to renew the charge, but as often the same deadly volley was poured in upon them with never-failing aim.

At length they attempted to set the thicket on fire, hoping thus to burn out their foes. There was another and still larger body of trappers about six miles below the point where this battle was raging But the direction of the wind was such, together with the dense forest and the broken ground, that the report of the fire-arms was not heard.

It is probable that the Indians had knowledge of this band, and feared that the larger party might come to the aid of their friends. Whatever may have been the reason which influenced them, they suddenly abandoned the contest and departed. As soon as Mr. Carson had satisfied himself that they were effectually out of the way, he emerged from his retreat and joined his friends down the river. His coolness and prudence had saved the party. They lost not a man nor an animal.

But the Indians still hovered around in such energetic and persevering hostility, that not a trapper could leave the camp without danger of falling into an ambuscade. The Indians avoided any decisive conflict, but their war-whoops and yells of defiance, like the howlings of wolves, could be heard, by day and by night, in the forests all around them. Unless the traps were carefully guarded, they were sure to be stolen. Under these circumstances there was no possibility of trapping with any hope of success. Once before the indomitable Indians had driven the trappers from their country. And now again it was deemed necessary to withdraw from their haunts.

To the trappers this was a very humiliating necessity. A council was held and it was decided to abandon the region and to direct their steps about two hundred miles, in a northeasterly direction, to the north fork of the Missouri river. The journey was soon accomplished without adventure. The trappers, far removed from their inveterate foes, vigorously commenced operations. They had their central camp. In small parties they followed up and down the majestic stream, and pursued the windings of the brooks flowing into it. They generally went in parties of two or three.

Wherever night found them, whether with cloudless skies or raging storm, it mattered not, the work of an hour with their hatchets, reared for them a sheltering camp. Before it blazed the ever-cheerful, illuminating fire. Rich viands of the choicest game smoked upon the embers, and the hunters, reclining upon their couches of blankets or furs, exulted in the luxurious indulgence of a hunter's life. With all the hardships to which one is exposed in such adventures, there is a charm accompanying them which words cannot easily describe. It warms the blood of one sitting upon the carpeted floor in his well-furnished parlor to send his imagination back to those scenes.

Men of little book culture, and with but slight

acquaintance with the elegancies of polished life, have often a high appreciation of the beauties and the sublimities of nature. Think of such a man as Kit Carson, with his native delicacy of mind; a delicacy which never allowed him to use a profane word, to indulge in intoxicating drinks, to be guilty of an impure action; a man who enjoyed, above all things else, the communings of his own spirit with the silence, the solitude, the grandeur, with which God has invested the illimitable wilderness; think of such a man in the midst of such scenes as we are now describing.

It is the hour of midnight. His camp is in one of the wildest ravines of the Rocky mountains. A dense and gloomy forest covers the hillsides. A mountain torrent, with its voice of many waters, flows on its way but a few yards beyond the open front of his camp. A brilliant fire illumines the wild scene for a few rods around, while all beyond is impenetrable darkness. His hardy mule, accustomed to all weathers, is browsing near by. The floor of his camp, spread with buffalo robes, looks warm and inviting. His two comrades are soundly asleep with their rifles on their arms, ready at the slightest alarm to spring to their feet prepared for battle.

There is a raging storm wailing through the treetops. The howling of the wolves is heard as, in fierce and hungry packs, they roam through these uninhabited wilds. Carson, reclining upon his couch, in perfect health and unfatigued, caresses the faithful dog, which clings to his side, as he looks out upon the scene and listens to the storm. What is there which the chambers of the Metropolitan hotel can afford, which the hardy mountaineer would accept in exchange?

Slowly our party of trappers ascended the river, gathering many furs on their way. It was an unexplored region, and they could never tell what scene the next mile would open before them. One morning as they were turning the majestic bend of a ravine, they came upon a beautiful little meadow, where the mountains retired for nearly a quarter of a mile from the stream, and where the waters of the river flowed gently in a smooth, untroubled current. They were ascending the river which flowed down from the south. A beautiful vista was opened before them of green valleys and gentle treeless eminences, while far away in the distance rose towering mountains.

Upon this lovely meadow there was a large village of Flathead Indians. Their conical lodges, constructed of skins, were scattered thickly around, while the smoke of their fires curled gently through an opening in the top of each lodge. Children were playing upon the greensward, shooting their arrows, throwing their javelins, and engaged in sundry other barbaric sports. A party of the Indians had just returned from a hunting expedition laden with game. Warriors and women were scattered around in small groups, discussing the events of the day and preparing for a great feast. Young Indian girls, of graceful form, looked very attractive in their picturesque attire of fringed buskined leggins and glittering beads.

Kit Carson at once recognized these Indians as his friends, the Flatheads. They knew him and gave him and his comrades a cordial greeting. O, the blessings of peace! How many are the woes of this world which are caused by man's inhumanity to man. The trappers were led by their Indian friends, with smiling faces and kind words, into their lodges, and shared with them in a thanksgiving feast.

Mr. Carson was endowed with unusual facility in the acquisition of languages. He could converse fluently in Spanish and French, and it was stated that he also understood some ten Indian dialects. With the Flatheads he was quite at home. After a few days, spent in this hospitable village, it was deemed expedient to seek winter quarters. Several of the chiefs accompanied them. They accordingly left the head waters of the Missouri, and crossed the Rocky mountains in a southerly direction, about two hundred miles, till they reached the Big Snake river. It will be remembered that this stream, flowing from the western declivities of the mountains, is the most important tributary of the Columbia river. Here the winter passed very pleasantly away without any incident which calls for record. Rather an unusual quantity of snow fell. But the trappers were warmly housed, with ample clothing and abundant fuel.

Every pleasant day hunters left the camp, and usually returned well laden with game. Thus the larder of the trappers was well provided for. An anonymous writer speaking of these winter encampments, says:

"The winter seasons in the Rocky mountains are usually fearful and severe. There snow-storms form mountains for themselves, filling up the passes for weeks and rendering them impracticable either for man or beast.

The scenery is indescribably grand, provided the beholder is well housed. If the case be otherwise, and he is doomed to encounter these terrible storms, his situation is dreadful in the extreme. Even during the summer months the lofty peaks of this mighty chain of mountains are covered with white caps of snow. It affords a contrast to the elements, of the grandest conception, to stand in the shade of some verdant valley wiping the perspiration from the brow, and at the same time to look upon a darkly threatening storm-cloud powdering the heads of the hoary monster mountains from its freight of flaky snow.

"So far these American giant mountains are unsurpassed by their Alpine brothers of Europe. Not so in the glaciers. Throughout the great range there are no glaciers to be found which can compare with those among the Alps."

In the spring the trappers scattered in small bands throughout that region. They were in the territory of the Utah Indians, just north of the Great Salt Lake. Kit Carson was well acquainted with them and they were all his friends. The trappers, therefore, wandered at pleasure without fear of molestation. Mr. Carson took but one trapper with him, with two or three pack mules. They were very successful, and in a few weeks obtained as many furs as their animals could carry.

With these they went to a trading post, not very far distant from them called Fort Robidoux. Here their furs were disposed of to good advantage. Mr. Carson, having judiciously invested his gains, organized another party of five trappers, and traversed an unpeopled wilderness for a distance of about two hundred miles until he reached the wild ravines and pathless solitudes of Grand river. This stream, whose junction with the Green river forms the Colorado, takes its rise on the western declivity of the Rocky mountains, amidst its most wild and savage glens. Trapping down this river with satisfactory success, late in the autumn he reached Green river. Falling snows and piercing winds admonished him that the time had come again to retire to winter quarters.

He repaired to Brown's Hole, the well known and beautiful valley which he had often visited before. Here he passed an uneventful but pleasant winter. With the earliest spring he again directed his footsteps to the country of the Utahs in the remote north. He was successful in trapping, and as the heat of summer came, he again turned his steps, with well laden mules, to Fort Robidoux. Here he found, to his disappointment, that beaver fur had greatly deteriorated in value. His skins would scarcely bring him enough to pay for the trouble of taking them. This was caused mainly by the use of silk instead of fur, throughout Europe and America, in the manufacture of hats.

Kit Carson saw at a glance, that his favorite occupation was gone; that he and the other trappers would be compelled to seek some other employment. In company with five men of a decidedly higher order than the common run of trappers, he struck for the head waters of Arkansas river. Following this stream down along the immense defile which nature seems to have opened for it through the Rocky mountains, they approached Fort Bent, which is about one hundred and fifty miles east of that gigantic barrier.

Mr. Carson's companions on this trip, were some of them at least, very peculiar characters,—very interesting specimens of the kind of men who are drawn from the haunts of civilization to the wilderness. One was a man, probably partially insane, who was known through all the Rocky mountain region as "old Bill Williams." He had been a Methodist preacher in Missouri. For some unknown reason he left the States and joined the Indians, adopting their dress and manners. He was very familiar with the Bible and had marvellous skill in the acquisition of languages. He would spend but a short time with any tribe before he became quite familiar with their speech. Though his conduct was often in strange contrast with the teachings of that sacred book, he took much pleasure in telling the Indians Bible stories. He was subsequently killed in some feud with the savages.

Another of his companions, whose real or assumed name was Mitchel, had abandoned his friends and joined the Comanche Indians. It is a much easier step from the civilized man to the savage than from the savage to the civilized. Mitchel, with his Indian costume, his plumed head-gear, his Indian weapons, and his fluent Indian speech, could not be distinguished from the savages around him. The Comanches adopted him into their tribe and accepted him as one of the most prominent of their braves. Mitchel said that his object was to discover a gold mine through their guidance, which they reported was to be found amid the mountains of Northern Texas. Disappointed in this endeavor, he joined the trappers and was cordially welcomed by them as an experienced mountaineer, a man full of humor and one who could tell a capital story.

When Kit Carson and his companions had arrived within a few days' journey of the fort, Mitchel and a man by the name of New, contrary to the advice of Carson, decided to remain behind, to enjoy themselves in a beautiful country where they found abundance of game. A week after the safe arrival of Mr. Carson and his party, these two men made their appearance in a truly pitiable plight. They had encountered a party of Indian hunters who, while sparing their lives, had robbed them of their arms, their ammunition and even of every particle of their clothing. Of course they were kindly received at the fort and all their wants supplied.

Fort Bent was a trading post; belonged to a com pany of merchants of whom Messrs. Bent and Vrain, residing at the fort, were partners. Immediately upon Mr. Carson's arrival there, he was so well known and his capabilities so well understood, that he received an earnest application to take the position of hunter for the fort. He accepted the office and filled it for eight years with such skill and fidelity that never did one word of disagreement pass between him and his employers. His duties were to supply a camp of about forty men with all the animal food they needed.

When game was plenty, this was an easy task, but often wandering bands of Indian hunters would sweep that whole region around rendering the labors of Mr. Carson extremely difficult. For unfrequently he would wander from sunrise to sunset over prairie and mountain, in pursuit of game; but rarely did he return without a mule load. At times he extended his hunting trips to a distance of fifty miles from the fort. During these eight years thousands of buffalo, elk, antelope and deer, fell before his rifle, besides a vast amount of smaller game.

The skill which he displayed, and the success which that skill secured, excited the admiration alike of the red men and the white men. He was universally known by the Indians, and was respected and beloved by them. Fearless and alone he wandered over mountain and prairie, frequently meeting bands of hunters, and warriors, and entering the lodges of the savages, and sleeping in them without encountering any harm. They admired his boldness, and an instinctive sense of honor led them not to maltreat one who had ever proved their friend, and who trusted himself so unreservedly in their power.

His familiarity with the Indian language enabled him to converse familiarly with them. He was as much at home in the wilderness as the most veteran hunters of their tribes. In the huts of the Arapahoes, Cheyennes, Kiowas and Comanches he was always a welcome guest. They appreciated the vast superiority of his intellect. Often groups of men, women and children would linger around the central fire of the lodge till after midnight, listening to his entertaining stories of adventure and peril.

One incident which occurred at this time, speaks volumes in reference to Mr. Carson's character as a lover of peace, and is deserving of perpetual remembrance.

The Sioux tribe of Indians who could bring a thousand warriors into the field had invaded the hunting-grounds of the Comanches. Several skirmishes had already taken place, in which the Comanches had been worsted. The chiefs sent a deputation to Kit Carson, whom they regarded as a host in himself, to come to their aid, and to take the leadership of one of their bands. Carson promptly responded to their call. He met the Comanche chiefs in council, and so represented to them the blessings of peace and the horrors of war, that they consented to send a deputation, to effect if possible, an amicable settlement of the difficulty.

We infer from the brief narrative that is given that Kit Carson was the bearer of this Indian flag of truce. He was the friend of both parties. He was alike regarded by both as eminent for his wisdom and his sense of justice. He met the Sioux chiefs in council. After long deliberation, they consented to retire from the Comanches' hunting-ground at the close of the then season, and never to molest them more.

Carson returned to the Comanches with this announcement, and persuaded them to accede to the terms. Thus a dreadful Indian war was averted.

Among some of these tribes Kit Carson found a beautiful and unusually intelligent Indian girl, whom he married, and took to his home in the fort.

It is the undisputed testimony of all who knew him, that he was a man of unspotted purity of character in his domestic relations. By this wife, Mr.

Carson had one child; a daughter. Not long after the birth of this child, the mother died. The father watched over the motherless infant with the utmost tenderness. As she emerged from infancy to childhood he removed her to St. Louis. Here he found the funds he had so carefully invested very valuable to him. He was able liberally to provide for all her wants, to give her as good an education as St. Louis could afford, and to introduce her to the refining influences of polished society. She was subsequently married and removed with her husband to California.

Sixteen years had now elapsed since Kit Carson left the log cabin of his father, in the then wilds of Missouri, for the still wilder regions of mountaineer life. Referring to this period, he says:

"During sixteen years my rifle furnished almost every particle of food upon which I lived. For many consecutive years, I never slept under the roof of a house, or gazed upon the face of a white woman."

He now, very naturally, began to long to visit the home of his childhood, and to witness some of the scenes of progressive civilization, rumors of which often reached him in the forest. Messrs. Bent and Vrain were in the habit of sending once a year a train of wagons to St. Louis, to transport their skins and to obtain fresh supplies. It was a journey of about six hundred miles. There was a wagon trail, if we may so call it, leading circuitously over the vast and almost treeless intervening plains. The route led along the river valleys, following the windings of streams, and conducting to fords near their head waters. Sometimes they came to swampy regions, sometimes to deep gulleys, sometimes to desert plains. But throughout all this wide expanse there were no mountain ranges to obstruct their path.

It was in the spring of the year 1842, that Mr. Carson, as a gentleman passenger, joined one of these caravans. The little daughter, of whom we have spoken, was then six or seven years of age. It was one object of his journey to place her at school, at St. Louis, where she could enjoy the advantages of a refined and christian education. We have no record of the incidents of this journey, which was probably uneventful. The old Indian trail had become quite a passable road for wagons.

## CHAPTER X.

### *Fremont's Expedition.*

**Carson's Visit to his Childhood's Home.—On the Steamer.—Introduction to Fremont.—Object of Fremont's Expedition.—Joins the Expedition.—Organization of the Party.—The Encampment.—Enchanting View.—Fording the Kansas.—The Stormy Night.—The Boys on Guard.—The Alarm.—The Returning Trappers.—The Homeless Adventurer.—Three Indians Join the Party.—First Sight of the Buffaloes.—The Chase.**

WHEN the caravan, with which Kit Carson travelled as a passenger from Fort Bent, arrived within the boundaries of Missouri, he left his companions and, with his little daughter, turned aside to visit the home of his childhood. He had, as we have mentioned, been absent from that home for sixteen years. Time, death, and the progress of civilization had wrought, in that region, what seemed to him fearful ravages. One of his biographers writes:

"The scenes of his boyhood days he found to be magically changed. New faces met him on all sides. The old log cabin where his father and mother had resided, was deserted and its dilapidated walls were crumbling with decay. The once happy inmates were scattered over the face of the earth, while many of their voices were hushed in death. Kit Carson felt himself a stranger in a strange land. The strong man wept. His soul could not brook either the change or the ways of the people. While he failed not to receive kindness and hospitality from the noble hearted Missourians, nevertheless he had fully allayed his curiosity and, as soon as possible, he bade adieu to these unpleasant recollections.

"He bent his steps towards St. Louis. In this city he remained ten days. As it was the first time, since he had reached manhood, that he had viewed a town of any magnitude, he was greatly interested. But ten days of sight-seeing wearied him. He resolved to return to his mountain home, where he could breathe the pure air of Heaven and where manners and customs conformed to his wild life and were more congenial to his tastes. He engaged a passage on the first steamboat which was bound up the Missouri river."

Kit Carson was instinctively a student. In whatever situation he was placed he was ever endeavoring to learn something new. He was also always drawn, by constitutional taste and preference towards men of culture, and high moral worth. On board the steamer, he found himself almost a perfect stranger. Though a small man in frame, modest and unobtrusive, there was something in his kindly handsome face and winning manners, which invariably attracted attention. As he quietly wandered over the boat, studying its machinery, the discipline of the crew and the faces of his fellow passengers, he found himself irresistibly drawn towards one whose countenance and dignified bearing indicated that he was decidedly above most of those on board.

It is said that "the eagle eye, the forehead, the form, the movements, the general features, the smile, the quiet dignity of the man, each and all these attributes of his manhood had been carefully noted by the wary and hardy mountaineer, and had not failed to awaken in his breast a feeling of admiration and respect."

Kit Carson entered into conversation with this man. Immediately an attachment sprang up between them, which grew increasingly strong through many subsequent years. The new friend whom Carson had thus found was Lieutenant John C. Fremont, of the United States corps of Topographical Engineers. He had been commissioned by the Government to explore and report upon the country between the frontiers of Missouri and the South Pass in the Rocky mountains, on the line of the Kansas and Great Platte rivers.

Lieutenant Fremont had left Washington, and arrived at St. Louis on the twenty-second of May 1842. Here he engaged a party of twenty-one men, principally Creole and Canadian boatmen, who were familiar with Indian life, having been long engaged in the service of the various fur companies. In addition to these boatmen, Lieutenant Fremont had under his charge, Henry Brandt, nineteen years of age, son of Colonel J. B. Brant, of St. Louis, and Randolph Benton, a lively boy of twelve years, son of the distinguished U. S. Senator from Missouri. These young men accompanied the expedition for that development of mind and body which their parents hoped the tour would give them.

With this party, Lieutenant Fremont was ascending the river four hundred miles, to the mouth of the Kansas, from which point he was to take his departure through the unexplored wilderness. We say unexplored, though many portions of it had been visited by wandering bands of unlettered trappers and hunters. Lieutenant Fremont had been disappointed in obtaining the guide he had expected. Upon learning this fact, Mr. Carson retired to a secluded part of the boat, sat down, and for some time seemed lost in reverie. Then rising and approaching Lieutenant Fremont he modestly said to him

"Sir, I have been for some time in the mountains, and think I can guide you to any point there you may wish to reach."

The office of a guide, through thousands of miles of untroden wilderness, was a very responsible position. Mr. Carson was an entire stranger to Lieutenant Fremont. But there was something in his bearing which inspired confidence. After making a few inquiries of others, Mr. Carson was engaged to act as guide with a salary of one hundred dollars a month.

The expedition commenced its march from near the mouth of the Kansas on the 10th of June 1842. It followed along the banks of that stream, in a westerly direction. The whole party consisted of twenty-eight souls. They were well armed and were well mounted with the exception of eight men, who drove as many carts. These carts were each drawn by two mules and were packed with the stores of the party, their baggage and their instruments. There were a number of loose horses in the train to supply the place of any, which might be disabled by the way. There were also four oxen, which were added as a contribution to their stock of provisions, one may well imagine that so numerous a cavalcade, winding its way over the undulating and treeless prairie, would present a very imposing aspect.

An Indian guide conducted them for the first

forty miles, along the river banks, with which Mr. Carson was not familiar. He then left them and they entered upon that vast ocean of prairie which extended, with scarcely any interruption, to the base of the Rocky mountains.

The borders of nearly all these western streams are fringed with a narrow belt of forest. Here where there was abundance of water, the richest of soil, which needed but to be "tickled with a hoe to laugh with a harvest," and where there was an ample supply of timber for building and for fuel, they found many good-looking Indian farms with Indians riding about in their picturesque costumes.

At an early hour in the afternoon they encamped in a smooth and luxuriant meadow, upon the banks of a small stream flowing into the Kansas. Nearly all the party were experienced backwoodsmen. Speedily, and with almost military precision, the camp was formed in the following manner: The eight carts were so arranged as to present a sort of barricade, encircling an area about eighty yards in diameter. The cloth tents, such as are used in the army, were pitched inside the enclosure. The animals were all hobbled and turned out to feed in the meadow. The company was divided into four messes of seven men each. Each mess had its cook. They quickly prepared the evening meal.

At nightfall all the animals, having been well fed on the abundant grass, were driven within the enclosure for the night and picketed. A small steel-shod picket was driven firmly into the ground, to which the animal was fastened by a rope about twenty feet long. The carts were regularly arranged for defending the camp. A guard was mounted at eight o'clock, consisting of three men, who were relieved every two or three hours. At daybreak the camp was roused. The hobbled animals were again turned loose upon the meadow or prairie to obtain their breakfast. The breakfast of the men was generally over between six and seven o'clock. The march was then resumed. There was a halt at noon for about two hours. Such was the usual order of the march day after day.

The second night, just as they were about to encamp, one of the loose horses started upon the full gallop, on his return, and was followed by several others. Several men were sent in pursuit. They did not return with the fugitives until midnight. One man lost his way and passed the whole night upon the open prairie. At midnight it began to rain violently. By some strange oversight, the tents were of such thin cloth that the rain soaked through, and those within them were thoroughly drenched. The discomfort of the night, however, was forgotten as the dawn of the morning ushered in another lovely summer day.

The journey through the beautiful and picturesque scenery was a delight. In the serene close of the afternoon they encamped on one of the Kansas bluffs. From this spot they had an enchanting view of the valley, about four miles broad, interspersed with beautiful groves and prairies of the richest verdure. This evening they killed one of their oxen for food. Thus far their route had been along the southern bank of the Kansas. The next day they reached what was called the ford of that river, a hundred miles from its entrance into the Missouri.

But the recent rains had so swollen the stream that it was rushing by, a swift and rapid torrent two hundred and thirty yards wide. The river could not be forded. Several mounted men entered it to swim their horses across, and thus to act as guides or leaders for the rest. The remaining animals were driven in, and all got safely across excepting the three oxen, who being more clumsy swimmers, were borne down by the current and again landed on the right side. The next morning, however, they were got over in safety.

Lieutenant Fremont had adopted the precaution of taking with him a portable India rubber boat. It was twenty feet long and five feet broad. It was placed in the water, and the carts and the baggage were carried over piecemeal. Three men paddled the boat. Still the current was so strong that one of the best swimmers took in his teeth the end of a rope attached to the boat and swam ahead, that, reaching the shore, he might assist in drawing her over. Six passages were successfully made and six carts with most of their contents were transported across. Night was approaching, and it was very desirable that everything should be upon the other side before the darkness closed in.

"I put," says Lieutenant Fremont, "upon the boat the two remaining carts. The man at the helm was timid on the water and, in his alarm, capsized the boat. Carts, barrels, boxes and bales were, in a moment, floating down the current. But all the men who were on the shore jumped into the water without stopping to think if they could swim, and almost everything, even heavy articles, was recovered. Two men came very near being drowned. All the sugar belonging to one of the messes was dissolved in the water and lost.

But the heaviest calamity of all was the loss of a bag containing the coffee for the whole company. There is nothing so refreshing to a weary mountaineer, as a cup of hot coffee. Often afterwards these travellers, overcome with toil, mourned the loss of their favorite beverage.

Kit Carson had made such efforts in the water, that in the morning he was found quite sick. Another of the party also was disabled. Lieutenant Fremont, on their account, and also to repair damages, decided to remain in camp for the day. Quite a number of the Kansas tribe of Indians visited them in the most friendly manner. One of them had received quite a thorough education at St. Louis, and could speak French as fluently and correctly as any Frenchman. They brought vegetables of various kinds, and butter. They seemed very glad to find a market for their productions.

The camping-ground of the party was on the open, sunny prairie, some twenty feet above the water, where the animals enjoyed luxuriant pasturage. The party was now fairly in the Indian country, and the chances of the wilderness were opening before them.

About three weeks in advance of this party, there was a company of emigrants bound to Oregon. There were sixteen or seventeen families, men women and children. Sixty-four of these were men. They had suffered severely from illness, and there had been many deaths among them. One of these emigrants, who had buried his child, and whose wife was very ill, left the company under the guidance of a hunter, and returned to the States. The hunter visited the Fremont camp, and took letters from them to their friends.

Day after day the party thus journeyed on, without encountering anything worthy of special notice. They had reached the Pawnee country. These savages were noted horse-thieves. The route of the surveyors led along the banks of a placid stream, about fifty feet wide and four or five feet deep. The view up the valley, which was bordered by gracefully undulating hills, was remarkably beautiful. The stream, as usual with these western rivers, was fringed with willows, cottonwood, and oak. Large flocks of wild turkeys tenanted these trees. Game, also, of a larger kind made its appearance. Elk, antelope and deer bounded over the hills.

A heavy bank of black clouds in the west admonished them, at an early hour in the afternoon, to prepare for a stormy night. Scarcely had they pitched their tents ere a violent wind came down upon them, the rain fell in torrents and incessant peals of thunder seemed to shake the very hills. It so happened that the three who were to stand guard on that tempestuous night, were Carson and the two young gentlemen Brandt and Benton.

" This was their first night on guard," writes Lieutenant Fremont "and such an introduction did not augur very auspiciously of the pleasures of the expedition. Many things conspired to render their situation uncomfortable. Stories of desperate and bloody Indian fights were rife in the camp. Our position was badly chosen, surrounded on all sides by timbered hollows, and occupying an area of several hundred feet, so that necessarily the guards were far apart. Now and then I could hear Randolph, as if relieved by the sound of a voice in the darkness, calling out to the sergeant of the guard, to direct his attention to some imaginary alarm. But they stood it out, and took their turn regularly afterwards."

The next morning, as they were proceeding up the valley, several moving objects were dimly discerned, far away upon the opposite hills; which objects disappeared before a glass could be brought to bear upon them. One of the company, who was in the rear, came spurring up, in great haste, shouting "Indians." He affirmed that he had seen them distinctly, and had counted twenty-seven. The party immediately halted. All examined their arms, and prepared for battle, in case they should be attacked. Kit Carson sprang upon one of the most fleet of the hunting horses, crossed the river, and galloped off, over the prairie, towards the hills where the objects had been seen.

"Mounted on a fine horse, without a saddle," writes Lieutenant Fremont, "and scouring, bareheaded, over the prairies, Kit was one of the finest pictures of a horseman I had ever seen. He soon returned quite leisurely, and informed them that the party of twenty-seven Indians had resolved itself into a herd of six elk who, having discovered us, had scampered off at full speed."

The next day they reached a fork of the Blue river, where the road leaves that tributary of the Kansas, and passes over to the great valley of the Platte river. In their march, across the level prairie of this high table-land, they encountered a squall of rain, with vivid lightning and heavy peals of thunder. One blinding flash was accompanied by a bolt, which struck the prairie but a few hundred feet from their line, sending up a column of sand.

A march of about twenty-three miles brought them to the waters of the majestic Platte river. Here they found a very delightful place of encampment near Grand Island. They had now travelled three hundred and twenty-eight miles from the mouth of the Kansas river. They had fixed the latitude and longitude of all the important spots they had passed, and had carefully examined the geological formation of the country.

They were working their way slowly up this

beautiful valley, to a point where it was only four miles wide. Here they halted to "noon." As they were seated on the grass, quietly taking their dinner, they were alarmed by the startling cry from the guard, of "All hands." In an instant everybody was up, with his rifle in hand. The horses were immediately both hobbled and picketed, while all eyes were directed to a wild-looking band approaching in the distance. As they drew near they proved to be a party of fourteen white men, returning on foot to the States. Their baggage was strapped to their backs. It was indeed a forlorn and way-worn band. They had, on a trapping excursion, encountered but a constant scene of disasters and were now returning to St. Louis, utterly impoverished.

They brought the welcome intelligence that buffaloes were in abundance two days' journey in advance. After a social hour, in which the two parties feasted together, the surveyors mounted their horses, and the trappers shouldered their packs, and the two parties separated in different directions. Lieutenant Fremont mentions an incident illustrative of the homeless life which many of these wanderers of the wilderness live:

"Among them," he writes, "I had found an old companion on a northern prairie, a hardened and hardly-served veteran of the mountains, who had been as much hacked and scarred as an old *moustache* of Napoleon's Old Guard. He flourished in the soubriquet of La Tulipe. His real name I never knew. Finding that he was going to the States, only because his company was bound in that direction, and that he was rather more than willing to return with me, I took him again into my service."

The company made but seventeen miles that day. Just as they had gone into camp, in the evening, three Indians were discovered approaching, two men and a boy of thirteen. They belonged to the Cheyenne tribe, and had been off, with quite a numerous band, on an unsuccessful horse-stealing raid among the Pawnees. Upon a summit, they had caught a glimpse of the white men, and had left their companions, confident of finding kind treatment at the camp-fires of the pale faces.

They were invited to supper with Lieutenant Fremont's mess. Young Randolph Benton, and the young Cheyenne, after eying each other suspiciously for some time, soon became quite intimate friends. After supper one of the Cheyennes drew, upon a sheet of paper, very rudely, but, as it afterwards appeared, quite correctly, a map of the general character of the country between the encampment and their villages, which were about three hundred miles further west.

The two next days the party made about forty miles. "The air was keen," writes Lieutenant Fremont, "the next morning at sunrise, the thermometer standing at 44 degrees. It was sufficiently cold to make overcoats very comfortable. A few miles brought us into the midst of the buffalo, swarming in immense numbers over the plains, where they had left scarcely a blade of grass standing. Mr. Preuss, who was sketching at a little distance in the rear, had at first noticed them as large groves of timber. In the sight of such a mass of life, the traveller feels a strange emotion of grandeur. We had heard, from a distance, a dull and confused murmuring, and when we came in view of their dark masses, there was not one among us who did not feel his heart beat quicker. It was the early part of the day when the herds are feeding, and every where they are in motion. Here and there a huge old bull was rolling in the grass, and clouds of dust rose in the air from various parts of the bands.

Shouts and songs resounded from every part of the line, and our evening camp was always the commencement of a feast which terminated only with our departure on the following morning. At any time of the night might be seen pieces of the most delicate and choicest meat, roasting on sticks around the fire. With pleasant weather, and no enemy to fear, an abundance of the most excellent meat and no scarcity of bread or tobacco, they were enjoying an oasis of a voyageur's life."

Three buffalo cows were killed to-day. Kit Carson had shot one, and was continuing the chase in the midst of another herd, when his horse fell headlong, but sprang up and joined the flying band. Though considerably hurt, he had the good fortune to break no bones. Maxwell, who was mounted on a fleet hunter, captured the runaway after a hard chase. He was on the point of shooting him, to avoid the loss of his bridle, a handsomely mounted Spanish one, when he found that his horse was able to come up with him.

The next day was the first of July.

As our adventurers were riding joyfully along, over a beautiful prairie country, on the right side of the river, a magnificent herd of buffalo came up from the water over the bank, not less then seven or eight hundred in number, and commenced slowly crossing the plain, grazing as they went. The prairie was here about three miles broad. This gave the hunters a fine opportunity to charge upon them before they could escape among the distant hills. The fleet horses for hunting, were brought up and saddled. Lieutenant Fremont, Kit Carson and L. Maxwell mounted for the chase. Maxwell was a veteran pioneer, who had been engaged as hunter for the expedition.

The herd were about half a mile distant from the company. The three hunters rode quietly along, till within about three hundred yards of the herd, before they seemed to be noticed by the buffaloes. Then a sudden agitation and wavering of the herd was followed by precipitate and thundering flight. The fleet horse can outstrip the buffalo in the race. The three hunters plunged after them at a hard gallop. A crowd of bulls, gallantly defending the cows, brought up the rear. Every now and then they would stop, for an instant, and look back as if half disposed to show fight.

"In a few moments," writes Lieutenant Fremont, "during which we had been quickening our pace, we were going over the ground like a hurricane. When at about thirty yards we gave the usual shout and broke into the herd. We entered on the side, the mass giving away in every direction in their heedless course. Many of the bulls, less fleet than the cows, paying no heed to the ground, and occupied solely with the hunters, were precipitated to the earth with great force, rolling over and over with the violence of the shock, and hardly distinguishable in the dust. We separated, on entering, each singling out his game.

"My horse was a trained hunter, famous in the west under the name of Proveau, and with his eyes flashing and the foam flying from his mouth, he sprang on after the cow, like a tiger. In a few moments he brought me along side of her. Rising in the stirrups, I fired, at the distance of a yard, the ball entering at the termination of the long hair, passing near the heart. She fell headlong at the report of the gun. Checking my horse, I looked around for my companions.

"At a little distance Kit was on the ground, engaged in tying his horse to the horns of a cow, which he was preparing to cut up. Among the scattered band, at some distance, I caught a glimpse of Maxwell. While I was looking, a light wreath of white smoke curled away from his gun, from which I was too far to hear the report. Nearer, and between me and the hills, towards which they were directing their course, was the body of the herd. Giving my horse the rein, we dashed after them. A thick cloud of dust hung upon their rear, which filled my mouth and eyes and nearly smothered me. In the midst of this I could see nothing, and the buffalo were not distinguishable until within thirty feet. They crowded together more densely still, as I came upon them, and rushed along in such a compact body that I could not obtain an entrance, the horse almost leaping upon them.

" In a few moments the mass divided to the right and left, the horns clattering with a noise heard above everything else, and my horse darted into the opening. Five or six bulls charged on us, as we dashed along the line, but were left far behind. Singling out a cow I gave her my fire, but struck too high. She gave a tremendous leap and scoured on swifter than before. I reined up my horse, and the band swept on like a torrent, and left the place quiet and clear. Our chase had led us into dangerous ground. A prairie-dog village, so thickly settled that there were three or four holes in twenty yards square, occupied the whole bottom for nearly two miles in length."

## CHAPTER XI.

*The Return of the Expedition.*

Beautiful Prairie Scene.—Fate of the Buffalo Calf.—Vast Buffalo Herds.—The Fourth of July on the Plains.—Journey up the South Fork of the Platte.—Visit to Fort St. Vrain.—Remonstrance of the Chiefs.—Second Marriage of Mr. Carson.—New Engagements.—Perilous Ride to Santa Fe.—The Successful Mission.—The Noble Mexican Boy.—Conflict with the Savage.—Discomfiture of the Indians.—Fremont's Second Expedition.—Carson joins the Party.—Course of the Expedition.—Arrival at the Great Salt Lake.

AFTER this exciting and successful buffalo hunt, the caravan in a long dark line advanced over the prairie twenty-four miles, and encamped on the banks of a stream, where they feasted abundantly upon the choicest cuts of buffalo beef. Wolves were howling around them all night, their instinct teaching them that bones would be left there which they would be privileged to gnaw. In the morning the wolves were seen sitting around at a short distance, barking and growling impatiently, waiting for the departure of the caravan.

Resuming their march, they ascended the stream about eighteen miles, where they found a fording-place and crossed over to the northern bank. Here there opened before them a rich and beautiful prairie, bordered with gentle eminences on the north and the south. This prairie extended about twenty miles along the banks of the river and was nearly six miles wide Its vast expanse was almost as smooth as a gentleman's lawn, and was waving with a luxuriant growth of grass and flowers. The river was skirted with a slight fringe of willow and cottonwood trees.

As Lieutenant Fremont intended to return by the same route, he concealed here for his homeward journey, in what is called a *cache*, a barrel of pork. They encamped in the evening upon the open prairie. As there was no wood at hand, they built their fires of the dry excrement of the buffalo. This substance, which was called buffalo chips, burns like turf and forms a very good substitute for wood. Immense numbers of wolves surrounded the camp at night, with an incessant and hideous howling and barking. In the morning, while the explorers were sitting quietly at breakfast, a small buffalo calf rushed frantic with terror through the camp, pursued by two wolves. The helpless little thing, separated from the herd, had probably mistaken the animals of the caravan for a herd of buffaloes. The frightened creature, discovering its error, continued its precipitate flight. The wolves, too wary to enter the camp, made a circuit around it, thus the calf got a little the start. It strained every nerve to reach a large herd of buffaloes at the foot of the hills, about two miles distant. Wolf after wolf joined in the chase until more than thirty were yelping in the hot pursuit.

A bull came out to the rescue of the little one, but was overpowered and driven back. Soon the foremost of the pack fastened their fangs into the calf, the rest were instantly upon him, and the quivering animal was pulled down, torn to pieces and devoured almost before he was dead. Every reader will sympathize with the remark of Lieutenant Fremont:

"We watched the chase with the interest always felt for the weak. Had there been a saddled horse at hand he would have fared better."

As the caravan was slowly advancing that afternoon, vast clouds of dust on their right near the hills attracted their attention. Several enormous herds of buffalo seemed to emerge from these clouds, galloping down towards the river. By the time the first bands had reached the water the whole prairie seemed darkened with the countless multitudes, numbering thousands upon thousands. They stretched in an unbroken line from the hills to the river, and fording the river passed on to the other side.

The prairie here was not less than two miles wide.

The mighty mass filled the whole expanse. As they reached the caravan, they circled around it leaving the travellers an open space of two or three hundred yards. The caravan continued its march, and the buffaloes continued their flow, until towards evening, when the company reached its camping-ground.

It was the evening of the fourth of July. All through the day preparations were being made to celebrate the anniversary by a great feast. Lieutenant Fremont gives the following attractive account of the bill of fare:

"The kindness of our friends at St. Louis had provided us with a large supply of excellent preserves and rich fruit cake. When these were added to macaroni soup and variously prepared dishes of the nicest buffalo meat, crowned with a cup of coffee, and enjoyed with prairie appetites, we felt as we sat in barbaric luxury around our smoking supper on the grass, a greater sensation of enjoyment than the Roman epicure at his perfumed feast. But most of all it seemed to please our Indian friends who, in the unrestrained enjoyment of the moment, demanded to know if our medicine days came often."

The party had now reached near the point where the north and south fork of the Platte river unite. Lieutenant Fremont wished to explore the south branch, to obtain some astronomical observations, and to determine the mouths of its tributaries, as far as St. Vrain's fort. He also hoped to obtain some mules there which he greatly needed. He took with him nine men. The three Cheyenne Indians accompanied him, as their village was upon that stream. The remainder of the company followed up the north fork to Fort Laramie to be joined by their companions there.

The journey proved an arduous one. It was intolerably hot; there were frequent tempests, with floods of rain and violent gusts of wind. The bottom lands on each side of the river seemed absolutely covered with buffaloes. Upon ascending any eminence vast herds were seen grazing as far as the eye could reach. Our adventurers pressed on, quietly and cautiously, following the windings of the stream. On the fourth day they discovered Indians in the distance; a band of three hundred, well mounted. Maxwell recognized the chief. This secured for them a friendly reception. They were led into their village. It consisted of a hundred and twenty-five lodges bordering a broad irregular street.

After a hospitable entertainment, they continued their journey and encamped in a little grove of cottonwood, in a cold drizzling rain. The next morning they caught their first glimpse of the Rocky mountains, about sixty miles distant. That day they came across a camp of four or five white men who were on a trapping expedition. They had all taken Indian wives, and a large number "of little fat buffalo-fed boys were tumbling about the camp, all apparently of the same age, about three or four years old." Their camp was on a rich bottom, luxuriant with grass, and they had many well fed horses and mules.

They reached St. Vrain's fort on the tenth, where they were hospitably received by Mr. St. Vrain. They purchased several horses and mules, and hired three additional men to accompany them across the country, one hundred and twenty-five miles, to Fort Laramie. On the twelfth they recommenced their journey, and reached the fort on the fifteenth. This trading post was quite an imposing military construction, with large bastions at the corners, its lofty walls being whitewashed and picketed. A cluster of lodges of Sioux Indians was pitched almost under the shadow of its wall. The party which Kit Carson had accompanied had arrived a few days before, and was encamped near by.

Here Fremont received the alarming intelligence that there was great excitement among the Indians beyond. They were all assuming a hostile attitude. Several parties of whites had already been cut off and massacred. Most of the men, at the Fort, remonstrated against his advance till the country should be somewhat settled. Even Kit Carson, though perfectly ready himself to proceed, declared his conviction that the danger was imminent, and that some encounters with the Indians were inevitable. He made his will, left it at the fort and was prepared to go.

Just before starting, the Sioux chiefs encamped at the fort almost forced themselves into Lieutenant Fremont's presence and presented him the following remonstrance written in good French:

"Mr. Fremont:

"The chiefs, having assembled in council, have just told me to warn you not to set out before the party of young men, which is now out, shall have returned. They tell me that they are sure they will fire upon you as soon as they meet you. They are expected back in seven or eight days. Excuse me for making these observations, but it seems my duty to warn you of danger. Moreover the chiefs, who prohibit your setting out before the return of the warriors, are the bearers of this note. I am your obedient servant,

"JOSEPH BISSONNETTE."

The chiefs who brought this note, four in number, sat in silence until it had been read. One of them rose and stepping forward shook hands with Mr. Fremont, and then said:

"You have come among us at a bad time. Some of our people have been killed, and our young men, who are gone to the mountains, are eager to avenge the blood of their relations, which has been shed by the whites. Our young men are bad. If they meet you they will believe that you are carrying goods and ammunition to their enemies, and will fire upon you. You have told us that this will make war. We know that our great father has many soldiers, and big guns, and we are anxious to have our lives. We love the whites and are desirous of peace. Thinking of all these things, we have determined to keep you here until our warriors return."

The others followed in the same strain. Lieutenant Fremont had the pride of an American military officer, and was not disposed to be driven from his course by threats of danger. He also believed the stories of peril to be greatly exaggerated, and that the great object of the chiefs was to prevent him from going farther into their country, where he had openly avowed it was his intention to establish a military fort. He therefore, in reply, urged that two or three of the chiefs should accompany him until they should meet the young men He said they should eat at his table and sleep in his tent, and that he would abundantly reward them on their return.

This they declined to do, saying that they were too old for such a journey.

Mr. Fremont then said to them, "You say that you love the whites. But you are unwilling to undergo a few days' ride to save our lives. We do not believe you. We will not listen to you. We are the soldiers of the great chief your father. He has told us to come here and see this country, and all the Indians. We shall not go back. We are few and you are many. You may kill us all. But do you think that our great chief will let his soldiers die and forget to cover their graves? Before the snows melt, his warriors will sweep away your villages as the fire does the prairie in the autumn. See! I have pulled down my white houses, and my people are ready. When the sun is ten paces higher, we shall be on the march."

They left the fort on the twenty-second of July, and followed up the north fork of the Platte for three weeks, encountering no molestation from the Indians, and meeting only with the ordinary hardships to be expected in travelling through the wilderness. They generally found a sufficiency of water, of grazing and of game. They at length found themselves among the wildest ravines of the Rocky mountains. Here they employed themselves day after day in astronomical and geological observations, and then commenced their return. All the objects of their expedition had been successfully accomplished. They reached Fort Laramie early in September. Kit Carson's labors were now ended. He had joined the expedition as hunter and guide. In neither of these offices were his services any longer required. He therefore remained at the fort, while the surveying party returned to St. Louis.

Mr. Carson's Indian wife had long been dead. Four months after this, in February, he married a Mexican lady, named Senora Josepha Jarimilla. This lady was highly esteemed by all who knew her for her many virtues, and was also endowed with much personal beauty. She subsequently became the mother of three children, for whom Mr. Carson has ever manifested the strongest attachment.

Two months after his marriage he engaged as a hunter to accompany an expedition of Messrs. Bent and Vrain's wagons to the United States. When about half-way across the plains, they struck the great Santa Fe trail. Here Carson and his companions came upon an encampment of Captain Cook, with four companies of U. S. Dragoons. They were escorting a train of Mexican wagons, as far as the boundary line between the United States and New Mexico. The region was infested with robber bands and it was deemed important that the richly freighted caravan should not encounter harm within the limits of the United States.

The Mexicans were apprehensive that, as soon as they should separate from their American protectors, they should be attacked upon entering Texas, by a large body of Texan Rangers, who, it was reported, were waiting for them. They therefore offered Kit Carson, with whose energetic character they were well acquainted, three hundred dollars, if he would carry a letter to Armijo the governor of New Mexico, who resided at Santa Fe. This letter contained an application to the governor to send them an escort. To convey the letter required a journey of between three and four hundred miles through a wilderness, filled with hostile Indian bands.

Carson accepted the offer, and engaging another man, Owens, to accompany him, rode back to Fort Bent. Here he learned that the Indians, through whose territory he must pass, were all up in arms against the whites, and that the journey would be full of peril. Owens refused to go farther. Carson was not a man to turn from duty because of danger. He found no one at the fort who could be induced to share the peril with him. He therefore set out alone. In addition to the powerful horse which he rode, Colonel Bent furnished him with a magnificent and fleet steed, which he led as a reserve corps.

Very rapidly Carson pressed on his way, watching for Indian trails and carefully avoiding all their wandering bands. From every eminence he narrowly examined the wide and generally treeless expanse spread out before him, in search of any sign of the foe. One afternoon he saw, far away in the distance, an Indian encampment of many lodges, directly on his trail. He immediately sought an out of the way place, where he might effectually secrete himself until night. When darkness came on, he, by a circuitous route, passed the camp of the savages and pressed rapidly on his way. In a few days he reached Taos, much exhausted by his impetuous ride.

He immediately called upon the mayor of the town, to whom he delivered the dispatches, and he at once sent an agent with them, down south a distance of about thirty miles to the governor at Santa Fe. He waited at Taos the return of the messenger to recruit himself and horses in preparation for his ride back. The response was that Governor Armijo had sent a hundred Mexican dragoons to seek the caravan, and that he was about to follow with six hundred more. We may mention in passing, that this company of one hundred men, were attacked after a few days' march, by a large body of Texan rangers, and were all massacred except one, who escaped on a fleet horse.

Governor Armijo and his dragoons, as they were on their way, learned of this massacre, and hearing exaggerated reports of the strength of the Texan Rangers, retreated rapidly to their fortification at Santa Fe. The governor, in the meantime, entrusted dispatches to Carson, thinking that he, by riding express, could reach the caravan before the governmental troops could come to their aid.

Carson was a remarkable judge of character. He selected, as a companion for his return, a Mexican boy whose innate nobility was soon developed. When two days out from Taos, Carson and his young companion came suddenly upon four Indian warriors. There was no escape, for the warriors, though at a distance, had seen them, and were riding rapidly down upon them. This noble young Mexican promptly turned to Kit Carson and said, "I am but a boy and perhaps the Indians will spare my life. At any rate your life is much more valuable than mine. Therefore mount the horse you are leading without delay, and you can undoubtedly make your escape."

Kit Carson replied, "I cannot and I will not forsake you. We must stand our ground together. If we have to die, let us take each with us an Indian warrior."

At this time the Indians had come near and halted out of rifle range, as Carson and his companion were taking deliberate aim at them, thus forbidding a nearer approach. One of the savages then alighted, and leaving his arms behind him, came forward for a parley. He assumed to be very much at his ease, and approached with a careless, swaggering air and a smile, and offered his hand in token of friendship. Carson accepted the proffered hand. The moment it was released, the savage, a man of herculean frame, grasped his rifle endeavoring to wrench it from him, doubtless intending instantly to shoot him down, when the boy would easily become their captive. But Carson, with his clenched fist and sinewy arm, gave the Indian instantly such a blow between the eyes as rolled him prostrate upon the grass, with the blood spouting from his nostrils.

The Indian, apprehensive that the next moment a rifle ball would pierce his heart, sprang up and with the fleetness of an antelope rejoined his companions. They were on the open prairie. There was nothing to afford either party the slightest protection. The Indians slowly and cautiously advanced, until they came within speaking distance. Carson, who could speak their language, hailed them and ordered them to stop. He then assured them, that if they advanced any farther or made any hostile demonstration whatever, two of their number would certainly and instantly die.

The savages began to bluster, primed their guns, and boasted of what they intended to do. But even to their darkened minds it was manifest that two out of the four, in case of hostilities, must certainly fall before the rifles of the white man. And should the remaining two rush on before their opponents could reload, still the white men had their revolvers in hand, and it was not improbable that the other two might be shot. These were not the circumstances under which the Indians were willing to enter into battle. After a short delay and many defiant gestures, they departed.

Mr. Carson and his noble-hearted boy immediately resumed their journey, and after five days of hard riding reached Fort Bent. Here Mr. Carson learned that the Texan Rangers, having incautiously entered the territory of the United States, were all captured and disarmed. This relieved the conductors of the Mexican train from all anxiety. The dispatches which Mr. Carson had borne were left at the fort, from which place they were sent back to Santa Fe.

A few days before Mr. Carson arrived at Bent's Fort, from this expedition into New Mexico, Mr. Fremont had passed by, on a second expedition to the still far off west. Carson was anxious to see his old friend and comrade again. He mounted his horse and, following his trail, by rapid riding overtook him after a pursuit of seventy miles. Colonel Fremont manifested the greatest pleasure in again meeting Mr. Carson, and so urged him to join the expedition that he decided to do so. It had become manifest that the party needed more mules to assist them in their operations. In climbing wild mountains these hardy animals are far more valuable than horses.

Kit Carson was sent back to Fort Bent to procure the mules, and to rejoin the party at St. Vrain's Fort, on the south fork of the Platte. Here Major Fitzpatrick, with a reinforcement of forty men, was added to the expedition. On Mr. Carson's return with the mules, the exploring party was divided into two forces; the main body, under Major Fitzpatrick, following the eastern bank of the river to the site of the present city of Denver, and then west, through the passes of the mountains. They took with them nearly all the camp equipage.

Colonel Fremont, with Kit Carson as a guide, accompanied by fifteen men, in what may be called light marching order, followed along the Thompson river some miles, directly west, then struck north about thirty miles, to the Cache le Poudre river. This stream they followed up in a northwesterly direction some sixty miles, through a ravine in the mountains, till they reached the head waters of the Laramie river. They then pushed on in a still northwesterly direction, under the eastern brows of the Rocky mountains, through a somewhat broken, though prairie country, two hundred miles, to the Sweetwater river.

They then pressed on, two or three hundred miles directly west, through the south pass of the Rocky mountains, along the route now followed by the Central Pacific Railroad, to Soda Springs, on Bear river. From this point Kit Carson was sent, with one companion and a relay of mules, about forty miles in a northwesterly direction to Fort Hall, on Snake river, to obtain supplies. He was directed to meet the remaining party at the extreme end of the Great Salt Lake. As usual he successfully accomplished his mission and rejoined his companions.

The whole body then journeyed down the eastern shores of this immense inland sea, about twenty miles. They were delighted with the beauty of the scenery opening before them, and were very busy in taking observations and exploring the country through which they passed. Far out in the lake there was seen a very attractive and densely wooded island. Colonel Fremont had with him an india rubber boat, which, with inflated air chambers, was very buoyant. Improvidently the plates of the boat had been gummed together only, instead of being also sewed. Thus the boat was very frail and could not endure the strain of a heavy sea.

It was the latter part of August, 1843, when Colonel Fremont encamped on these shores. Though this was but thirty years ago, that now quite populous region, had then been visited only by trappers in search of beaver streams. Colonel Fremont decided to visit the island. He selected a pleasant spot for encampment, in a grove on one of the banks of Bear river, near its entrance into the lake. He felled timber so as to make a large pen for the animals. He then erected a rude fort, which would protect the company from any ordinary band of Indians. The boat was repaired with gum, and the air chambers inflated. Game was found to be scarce, and their provisions were about exhausted. He therefore sent back one half his party to Fort Hall for supplies.

Leaving two or three to guard the fort and the horses, Colonel Fremont, with Carson and three other men, set out on their expedition to explore the island. It was a very beautiful morning, the eighth of September. Slowly they floated down the romantic stream, frequently stopping to get a shot at the wild geese and ducks they met on their way. It was not until the edge of the evening that they reached the outlet of the river.

They encamped in a small willow grove, where they found an abundance of drift-wood for their camp fire. The game they had taken furnished their supper. They made for themselves soft beds of the tender willow twigs, and in a mild atmosphere, beneath a starlit sky, slept soundly till morning. The voices of millions of waterfowl, around them, did not disturb their slumbers.

## CHAPTER XII.

### *Marches and Battles.*

Entering the Lake.—Dangerous Navigation.—The Return to Camp.—Feast upon Horse Flesh.—Meeting the Indians.—Joyful Meeting.—Return to Fort Hall.—Feasting at the Fort.—The Party Diminished.—The Journey down Snake River.—Crossing the Sierra Nevada.—Carson Rescues Fremont.—Fort Sutter.—Heroic Achievement of Carson.—Disbanding the Party.—The third Expedition.—Crossing the Desert.—Threatened by the Mexicans.—Fight with the Indians.—The Surprise.—Chastisement of the Indians.

THE morning of the ninth of September dawned upon our voyagers remarkably serene and beautiful. They hurried through breakfast to make an early start. The water was found so shallow, at the mouth of the river, that it would not float the boat. They were compelled to take off their clothes and wade through the soft mud for the distance of a mile, dragging the boat, when they came to deep water. The whole wide marshy expanse seemed to be covered with waterfowl of every description, filling the air with their discordant voices. Though it was calm, there was quite a heavy swell upon the ocean-like lake. The waters were of crystal clearness, though so thoroughly saturated with salt that the spray left a saline crust upon the clothing.

They reached the island and ascended its loftiest peak, which was about eight hundred feet high. It is almost certain that never since the creation had a white man's foot trod that summit.

"As we looked," writes Colonel Fremont, "over the vast expanse of water spread out beneath us, and strained our eyes along the silent shore, over which hung so much doubt and uncertainty, I could hardly repress the desire to continue our exploration. But the lengthening snow on the mountains, spreading farther and farther, was a plain indication of the advancing season, and our frail linen boat appeared so insecure that I was unwilling to trust our lives to the uncertainties of the lake. I therefore unwillingly resolved to terminate our survey here and to remain satisfied for the present with what we had been able to add to the unknown geography of the region. We felt also pleasure in remembering that we were the first who, in the traditionary annals of the country, had visited the island and broken with the cheerful sound of human voices, the long solitude of the place.

"Out of the drift-wood on the beach, we made ourselves pleasant little lodges, open to the water, and, after having kindled large fires, to excite the wonder of any straggling savage on the lake shores, lay down, for the first time in a long journey, in perfect security, no one thinking about his arms. The evening was extremely bright and pleasant. But the wind rose during the night, and the waves began to break heavily, making our island tremble. I had not expected, in our inland journey, to hear the roar of an ocean surf. The strangeness of our situation, and the excitement we felt, in the associated interests of the place, made this one of the most interesting nights I remember during our long expedition."

The next morning they set out at an early hour, on their return to the main land, about nine miles distant. When they had rowed about three miles the clouds gathered, menacing a storm, and a strong wind rose, blowing directly against them. The heavy sea which they encountered caused a leakage in the air chambers of the boat, and they were in imminent danger of finding a grave in the bottom of the lake. It was with much difficulty that a man, stationed at the bellows, supplied the chamber with air as fast as it escaped.

At length they effected a landing on marshy ground, about nine miles from the encampment. Two men were immediately dispatched to the camp to bring horses to take back the boat and baggage.

" The rude looking shelter," writes Colonel Fremont, "we raised on the shore, our scattered baggage and boat lying on the beach made quite a picture. We called this the fisherman's camp."

The horses arrived in the afternoon. It was then blowing such a gale that a man could hardly stand against it. The water of the lake was rapidly rising, forced in by the wind. Very hurriedly they packed their baggage and had scarcely left the spot ere it was entirely submerged. They reached the camp in the edge of the evening, just in time to escape a thunder storm, which blackened the sky and deluged the earth with rain. The next day they remained at the camp, and boiled down five gallons of lake water which yielded fourteen pints of very fine white salt. The ensuing morning was calm and beautiful, as is almost invariably the case during the summer and autumnal months, throughout all that region.

They now commenced their return by the same route they had already traversed, ascending the valley of the Bear river towards the north. Day after day they journeyed on, without meeting much game, and their supply of food was nearly exhausted. All the party seemed low-spirited, and trudged along in silence. Scarcely a word was spoken. On the night of the fourteenth they encamped on the bank of a crystal stream. It was a lovely evening, serene and mild. But the company seemed very forlorn from hunger. Colonel Fremont therefore consented that a fat young horse, which he had purchased of the Indians, should be killed for food. As the company gathered around their brilliant camp-fires, feasted on the savory horse steak, the customary good-humor and gayety were restored.

The next day, as they were still ascending the valley, they came upon two families of Snake Indians who were gathering herbs and roots. The berries they were drying on buffalo robes. These two families had twelve or fifteen horses grazing around their encampment. Soon after this they encountered a solitary Indian, who had an antelope which he had killed. They purchased the antelope and encamped early to enjoy the rich feast. While they were protracting the pleasures of their repast, a messenger came galloping into their camp saying that Mr. Fitzpatrick was within a few miles of them, with an ample supply of provisions. They could scarcely sleep that night for joy. The next morning before sunrise they were on the move and soon rejoined their friends. Together they continued their journey to the northward, encountering several lodges of Snake Indians; of whom they purchased about a bushel of dried berries.

Leaving the valley of the Bear river they crossed over to Snake river, or as it is sometimes called,

Lewis's Fork of the Columbia river. On their way they met an Indian family on horseback, who had been gathering what are called service berries. At night fires were seen burning all along the mountain-sides, indicating numerous encampments of the Indians. But they were all friendly, and the weary voyagers slept with a very happy and grateful sense of security. On the eighteenth they entered the spacious valley of the Snake river, near its upper waters. The next morning the snow began to fall and it continued snowing all day.

They were now very near Fort Hall. They therefore encamped, and Colonel Fremont rode up to the fort and purchased several horses, and five fat oxen. The arrival of the oxen, giving promise of such good cheer, was received with shouts of joy. Though night came down upon the wanderers, cold and stormy, rousing fires and smoking steaks made all happy.

For several days the party remained in their encampment. They had journeyed from the frontier of Missouri, thirteen hundred and twenty-three miles. Though winter had come on thus early, and both game and forage were known to be scarce along the route they were about to travel, Colonel Fremont decided to continue his explorations, regardless of ice and cold. He thought it, however, expedient to diminish the number of his party. Accordingly he assembled the men, informed them of his intention, and of the great hardships to which they would doubtless be exposed. Thus he persuaded eleven men to withdraw from the expedition, and return to the States.

With the lessened party, about twenty in number, Colonel Fremont recommenced his journey, on the twenty-second of September, down the valley of the river towards the mouth of the Columbia. We have not space here to record the many interesting events of this journey. The Colonel bears constant and affectionate testimony to the services rendered by Kit Carson. After travelling six or seven hundred miles, they reached Fort Dalles, then passing directly south, through the very heart of the Oregon territory, they made a thorough exploration of Klamath Lake, to its extreme southern border.

Thence they started for California. It was necessary to cross a ridge of the Sierra Nevada mountains. The snow was six feet deep on a level. The toils and sufferings of the men were dreadful. There was neither game nor forage to be found. Many of the mules died of starvation. One incident, which occurred during this dreadful march, we give in the words of Colonel Fremont. Under date of February 23d he writes:

"This was our most difficult day. We were forced off the ridges, by the quantity of snow among the timber, and obliged to take to the mountain sides, where occasionally rocks and a southern exposure afforded us a chance to scramble along. But these were steep, and slippery with snow and ice, and the tough evergreens of the mountain impeded our way, tore our skins, and exhausted our patience. Some of us had the misfortune to wear moccasins, with soles of buffalo hide, so slippery that we could not keep our feet, and generally we crawled along the snow beds. Axes and mauls were necessary to make a road through the snow.

"Going ahead with Carson, to reconnoitre the road, we reached, this afternoon, the river which made the outlet of the lake. Carson sprang over, clear across a place where the stream was compressed among the rocks. But the sole of my moccasin glanced from the icy rock, and precipitated me into the river. It was some few seconds before I could recover myself in the current, and Carson thinking me hurt, jumped in after me, and we both had an icy bath. We tried to search a while for my gun, which had been lost in the fall, but the cold drove us out. Making a large fire on the bank, after we had partially dried ourselves, we went back to meet the camp. We afterwards found that the gun had been slung under the ice which lined the shores of the creek."

Upon reaching the southern declivity of the mountains, Fremont and Carson, with six others, pushed ahead to Fort Sutter where, it will be remembered, the gold of California was first discovered. The whole party reached the fort on the sixth of March, 1844. These extraordinary men, in the depths of winter, had travelled from Fort Hall about two thousand miles. They remained at the Fort recruiting but a fortnight. A braver enterprise history does not record. Its successful accomplishment sent the name of John C. Fremont, its leader, on the wings of fame, throughout the civilized world. We have no space to record the vastly important results accomplished by this exploration.

Upon leaving the fort, on their return towards the States, they met a Mexican and a little boy, who were in great destitution and grief. They had been left with a band of six, among whom were the boy's father and mother, to watch their animals grazing in a fertile meadow. They were suddenly attacked by a party of thirty Indians, who either captured or killed all of the party except the man and the boy, who fortunately escaped. The Indians fled with their booty. The poor boy was overwhelmed with grief.

He had every reason to fear that both of his parents were dead.

Kit Carson's heart was touched. He proposed to Richard Godoy, an experienced and noble-hearted mountaineer, that they two should pursue the thirty Indian warriors, rescue the captives, and regain the animals. They soon struck the Indian trail and followed it nearly all the night. The Indians, not apprehensive of pursuit, were travelling leisurely. Towards morning, Carson and his companion halted for an hour or two, to allow their horses to graze and to get a little sleep. At daybreak they were again in the saddle, and just at sunrise discovered the Indians in a snug little valley, feasting luxuriously upon horse-steaks. They had already killed five of the stolen animals.

These two men immediately charged, with a loud shout, upon the thirty warriors. The savages were taken utterly by surprise, and thrown into a panic. Carson's practiced eye selected the chief, who instantly fell pierced through the heart by a bullet from Carson's rifle. Godoy missed his aim, but instantly reloading, another warrior dropped in his blood. The Indians, not doubting that the two were but the advance party of a strong force, fled with precipitation, abandoning everything. Deliberately Carson collected the horses, counted them and found that they had them all, excepting the five the thieves had killed.

They then followed the trail back to the spot where the savages had attacked the Mexicans. The captives had all been killed and their bodies had been shockingly mangled. Carson and his heroic companion, with fifteen horses, rejoined the camp. The property was at once restored to the Mexicans without any remuneration whatever being received by either of these men for their exploit. They had been absent from the camp thirty hours, and had ridden over a hundred miles.

The march was now resumed and, after a tedious journey of many leagues, they reached Fort Bent on the second of July, where the exploring party was disbanded. Colonel Fremont proceeded to Washington. Kit Carson returned to Taos. Thinking that he had had enough of wandering, he decided to become a farmer, that he might reside at home with his family. He purchased quite a large tract of land a little out from the straggling village of Taos, and commenced farming upon a pretty large scale.

As he was very busy erecting his buildings and breaking up the soil, an express arrived from Colonel Fremont, stating that he was about to set out on a third exploring tour and that he should depend upon Mr. Carson's accompanying him. He also reminded him of a promise once given that he would be ever ready to heed such a call.

Mr. Carson had made large investments in buildings, stock, farming utensils, etc. With Mr. Owens, who had been his companion on a former trip, Mr. Carson set out for Fort Bent, where he met with a very cordial welcome from Colonel Fremont. We cannot follow the party, in its long and adventurous wanderings, along the ravines, across the prairies, and over the mountains, until they reached the lower extremity of the Great Salt Lake. Before them towards the west spread out a vast desert, of unknown extent. No white man had ever crossed it. Colonel Fremont decided that it was his duty to explore it. His men were always ready to follow their bold chieftain.

Kit Carson and three others were sent forward to mark out the road by their trail. Should they find grass and water, they were to build a fire, the smoke of which would convey the joyful intelligence to Colonel Fremont, who was watching, spy-glass in hand, from a neighboring eminence. For sixty miles they travelled without finding a drop of water, or a blade of grass. Then suddenly they came upon both in abundance; an oasis in the desert.

Carson built a rousing fire, piling on the green wood to make as much smoke as possible. Notwithstanding the great distance, the glass of Fremont discerned the billowy signal, ascending through the serene skies. His party was at once put in motion, and after a weary march reached their companions. They thence pressed on to Sutter's Fort, where they could only obtain moderate supplies. On the trip they had divided into two parties and one of them had wandered and got lost. Mr. Carson was sent to hunt them up. With his usual skill and promptitude, he accomplished his mission, and brought the lost party safely to the fort. They then directed their course to Monterey, on the sea coast, where they could obtain all they needed. When within thirty miles of the place, an express arrived from General Castro, the Mexican commander of the territory, ordering Colonel Fremont and his party to leave the country or he would compel them to do so.

Instead of obeying this order, Colonel Fremont, with but forty men under his command, immediately selected a good military position, and prepared for a defence. General Castro soon appeared with several hundred troops, infantry, cavalry and artillery, and established himself within a few hundred yards of the Fremont camp. The two parties watched each other for three days. Colonel Fremont then, satisfied that the Mexicans would not assume the offensive, and that it would be rash to attempt to force his way against so powerful a foe, turned his steps north to the Sacramento river, and thence to the mouth of the Columbia.

On the route they met a thousand Indian warriors. They were armed only with arrows and javelins. A fierce battle ensued. The Indians were repelled with heavy loss. Mr. Carson thinks that in that conflict, they became convinced that with their weapons, they could never hope to vanquish the rifle-armed white men. Upon this trip they also learned that war had broken out between the United States and Mexico. The express which brought this intelligence informed Fremont that a United States officer was in the rear, with a few men in imminent peril.

Colonel Fremont took Carson and ten other picked men, and hastened to the rescue. Mr. Carson himself gives the following account of a tragic scene which soon took place. The narrative was given in a letter published in the Washington Union of June, 1847:

"Mr. Gillespie had brought the Colonel letters from home and he was up, and kept a large fire burning until after midnight. This was the only night, in all our travels, except the one night on the island in Salt Lake, that we failed to keep guard.

As the men were so tired and we expected no attack now that we had sixty in the party, the Colonel did not like to ask it of them, but sat up late himself. Owens and I were sleeping together, and we were waked at the same time by the licks of the axe that killed our men. At first I did not know it was that, but I called to Basil who was on that side:

"What's the matter there? What's that fuss about?"

"He never answered for he was dead then, poor fellow, and he never knew what killed him. His head had been cut in, in his sleep. The Delawares, we had four with us, were sleeping at that fire, and they sprang up as the Klamaths charged them. One of them caught up a gun which was unloaded, but although he could do no execution he kept them at bay like a soldier, and did not give up till he was shot full of arrows, three entering his heart.

"As soon as I had called out I saw it was Indians in the camp, and I and Owens cried out together, 'Indians.' There were no orders given, things went on too fast, and the Colonel had men with him that did not need to be told their duty. The Colonel and I, Maxwell, Owens, Godey and Stepp jumped together and went to the assistance of our Delawares.

"I dont know who fired first and who didn't; but

I think it was Stepp's shot that killed the Klamath chief; for it was at the crack of Stepp's gun that he fell. He had an English half-axe slung to his wrist by a cord, and there were forty arrows left in his quiver; the most beautiful and warlike arrows I ever saw. He must have been the bravest man among them, from the way he was armed, and judging from his cap.

"When the Klamaths saw him fall, they ran; but we lay, every man with his rifle cocked, until daylight, expecting another attack. In the morning we found, by the tracks, that from fifteen to twenty of the Klamaths had attacked us. They had killed three of our men and wounded one of the Delawares, who scalped the chief, whom they left where he fell.

"Our dead men we carried on mules; but after going about ten miles we found it impossible to get them any farther through the thick timber. And finding a secret place we buried them under logs and chunks, having no way to dig a grave. It was only a few days before this, that some of these same Indians had come into our camp; and although we had only meat for two days and felt sure that we should have to eat mules for ten or fifteen days to come, the Colonel divided with them, and even had a mule unpacked to give them some tobacco and knives."

In consequence of the war declared between the United States and Mexico, Colonel Fremont thought it expedient to return to California. He judged it, however, to be necessary first, as a lesson to the savages, to punish them severely for their wanton murder of his men. Kit Carson, at the head of ten chosen mountaineers, was sent forward in search of their strongholds. If he discovered them without being seen himself he was to return for reinforcements. If seen he was to act as he thought best.

He soon discovered an Indian trail, and followed it to an Indian encampment of fifty lodges, containing one hundred and fifty warriors. The agitation in the camp evidenced that the Indians had obtained warning of danger. Carson decided to attack them instantly, in the midst of their confusion. The Indians for a moment made a bold stand. But as bullet after bullet pierced them, from the invisible missiles of their foe, whom they could not reach with arrows, they turned in a panic and fled. Mr. Carson wishing to inflict chastisement which would not soon be forgotten, ordered all their valuables to be collected in their lodges and then applied the torch. The flames leaped high in the air and in an hour nothing remained of the Indian village, but glowing embers and the bodies of their dead warriors.

Colonel Fremont saw the smoke of the conflagration and understood its significance. He hastened forward and joined Carson. But it was thought that the Indians had not yet received the punishment which their crime deserved. The whole party then moved on together for several miles, to a secluded encampment.

Mr. Carson said that the warriors would certainly return to view the ruins of their village and to bury their dead. Twenty men were consequently sent back to lie in ambush. At midnight fifty savages were seen in the bright moonlight, approaching their ruined homes. Some alarm caused them precipitately to retreat. Carson was a little in advance with Colonel Fremont. He saw one solitary warrior separate from the rest. Spurring upon the savage at the distance of not ten paces he endeavored to shoot him, when his gun missed fire. He was now apparently at the mercy of the Indian, who had already with sinewy arm, drawn an arrow to the feather to pierce the body of his foe.

Fremont was mounted on a very powerful and spirited charger. He plunged the rowels of his spurs into the animal, when the noble horse made one or two frantic leaps, knocked down the Indian and trampled over him. The arrow of the savage flew wide of its mark. The next moment a rifle ball pierced his heart, and he lay quivering in death.

The party now pressed on to the Sacramento river. The Klamath warriors dogged their path, watching for an opportunity to take them at advantage. One day Carson and Godey, who were a little separated from the rest of the company, came quite unexpectedly upon a band of these warriors and instantly charged upon them. One Indian only was too proud to fly. He took his position behind a rock and as soon as the two white men came within shooting distance, he let fly his arrows with great force and rapidity.

After dodging these arrows for some time, Carson mounted and crept through concealment, till he obtained good aim at the savage. There was a sharp report of the rifle, and the Indian was dead. Carson took from him a beautifully wrought bow and a quiver still containing a number of arrows. But the savages still continued to hover around their trail without venturing upon any attack.

## CHAPTER XIII.

### *The Dispatch Bearer.*

Colonel Fremont.—Hazardous Undertaking of Kit Carson.—Carson's Courage and Prudence.—Threatened Danger.—Interview with General Kearney, and Results.—Severe Skirmish.—Wonderful Escape of Carson.—Daring Adventure.—Fearful Suffering.—Lieutenant Beale.—Carson's Journey to Washington.—Adventures on his Return.

OUR explorers now pressed on for twenty-four hours without encountering any molestation, though they saw many indications that the Indians were hovering about their track. Hungry and weary, they reached Fort Lawson, on the Sacramento river, where they tarried for a week to recruit. They then followed down the river some distance, to the well-known camping-grounds, "The Buttes."

War between the United States and Mexico was in active operation. Colonel Fremont took the responsibility of capturing a weak Mexican post near by, at Sonoma, where he obtained several cannon and some small arms. His explorers being thus virtually resolved into an army, he marched, with Kit Carson as nominal Lieutenant, for the capture of Monterey.

Before he reached there, the city was taken by an American squadron under Commodore Sloat. Colonel Fremont obtained a ship to convey him, with his fast friend Kit Carson, and one hundred and fifty bold mountaineers, who had attached themselves to his fortunes, a few hundred miles down the coast, to San Diego. Thence he marched upon Los Angelos.

It was becoming important to have some communication with Washington. To send dispatches around by the cape, required a voyage of weary months. To reach the capital by land, it was necessary to traverse an almost pathless wilderness four thousand miles in extent. Whoever should undertake such an enterprise, must not only live upon such food as he could pick up by the way, but also be exposed to attack from innumerable bands of hostile savages, urged on by still more hostile Mexicans.

On the fifteenth of September, 1846, Kit Carson undertook this hazardous enterprise. He was placed in command of fifteen picked men. The utmost vigilance was necessary every step of the way. He was instructed to make the journey in sixty days. For two days, he pressed on his way without molestation. The third day, he came suddenly in view of a large encampment of Apache Indians. Each party discovered the other at the same moment. There was instantly great commotion in the Indian camp; the warriors running to and fro in preparation for a fight.

Mr. Carson, acquainted with their language, and also familiar with all their customs, saw at once that his only safety consisted in reckless courage. He halted his little band, and assuming an air of entire unconcern, rode forward till he came within speaking distance, and of course within arrow distance of hundreds of plumed and painted warriors. He was entirely at their mercy. They might instantly pierce him, and almost bury him beneath a shower of arrows. The chief of the white men being thus killed, the rest of the party would fall easily a prey to their overpowering numbers. Carson shouted out to them:

"I come to you as a friend, and I ask for a parley."

Two or three warriors then came forward and with the usual preliminaries, held a brief conference. They could without any difficulty have seized upon Carson and held him as a hostage. But he knew that his only possible safety was in this apparent act of desperation. Having smoked the pipe of peace, he said to them:

"We come to you as friendly travellers, seeking only a passage through your country. We come to you as brothers, presenting the olive branch of peace.

We do not wish to harm you. We ask only for your friendship. Our animals are weary. We would exchange them for those that are fresh. We will pay you well for the exchange."

If that be eloquence which moves the heart, this was eloquence. It changed the hearts of the Indians. Friendly demonstrations immediately took the place of preparations for a bloody fight. Carson pitched his camp at a short distance from the Apaches. His prudence, as well as his courage, was developed. He selected a site where in case of treachery, he could make a vigorous defence. Every man had rifle, revolver, and knife. Every man was instructed, while assuming an air of entire trust in the Indians, to be constantly on the watch. There was to be no surrender. In case of attack, every man was to sell his life as dearly as possible. The calm, self-possessed, invincible spirit of this wonderful man was infused into all his followers. Fifteen such men with rifles, revolvers, and knives, would make terrible havoc among a crowd of Indian warriors, before they could all be cold in death.

As soon as the camp was arranged, the Indians were allowed to come in. They smoked and feasted, and traded together, in the most friendly manner. Carson remounted all his men on fresh and vigorous steeds. The next morning he went on his way rejoicing.

Nearly a month passed away, as this heroic little band, with tireless diligence, pressed along their pathless route towards the rising sun. With the utmost caution, Mr. Carson avoided the Indian trails, making a path for himself. He would often make a wide circuit, that he might not cross hunting grounds where his experience taught him that Indian hunting bands would probably be encountered.

It was a bright and beautiful morning, the sixth of October, that they entered upon the western edge of a smooth, treeless prairie extending to the east as far as the eye could reach. Soon after the morning sun began to flood that ocean of waving flowers with its rays, the keen eye of Carson discerned in the extreme east, a small speck, like the sail of a ship at sea. He watched it, it moved. Slowly it increased in size. It soon developed itself into the front of a numerous band of warriors. His anxiety was great. It was not wise to attempt flight over the boundless prairie.

As the column drew nearer, he discovered to his great joy that it was a detachment of United States troops. The expedition had been sent out by the government, to operate under General Kearney, in California. As the two parties met, General Kearney sent for Mr. Carson, and after a little conversation with him, decided to entrust his dispatches to Mr. Fitzpatrick, to convey them to Washington, while he should attach Mr. Carson to his staff as a guide, of which he stood greatly in need. Upon informing Mr. Carson of this his decision, the modest reply of the pioneer was, "As the General thinks best."

Mr. Carson now was invested with the responsible office of guiding the footsteps of this army over these almost boundless plains. This duty he so performed as to receive the highest commendation of General Kearney. And his dignified character was such as to win the confidence and respect of every man in the army. The worst of men can often appreciate high moral excellence.

Early in December the army had reached California, and were approaching San Diego. On the sixth, the scouts brought the news that a numerous party of Mexicans were strongly intrenched a few miles before them, to dispute their passage. Fifteen men were sent forward as an advanced guard, under the guidance of Kit Carson, to drive in the outposts, and capture any loose animals which might be found. A very fierce battle ensued. These Californian Mexicans developed a degree of bravery and determination totally unexpected, and which could not have been exceeded.

Quite a number of troops had come up to assist in carrying an important post. In addition to the fifteen men with Carson, there were two companies of United States dragoons, and twenty-five California volunteers. These determined men, all well mounted, formed a very imposing column for the charge. Mr. Carson was in the front rank of the column. As the horses were plunging forward upon the foe, Mr. Carson's horse, from some inequality in the ground, fell, throwing his rider over his head with such violence as to break his gun-stock in several pieces. Carson was slightly stunned by the fall, and the whole troop of horse galloped over him. It seems a miracle that he was not trampled to death. Though severely bruised, no bones were broken.

Upon recovering, and finding his own gun useless, he looked around and saw a dead dragoon. Seizing his gun, he rushed forward into the thickest of the fight. It is probable that the fall of his horse saved his life. Nearly the whole of the head of the charging column was cut off by the bullets of the foe. The Mexicans were soon driven from their post, and fled on swift horses. But the Americans suffered terribly. Large numbers were killed.

The Mexicans soon rallied with reinforcements

and resumed the battle. The advanced guard of the Americans was driven back and compelled to act upon the defensive. We have not space here to give, in detail, the victories and defeats of these fierce conflicts. Most of these California Mexicans were of the bravest blood of Spain. And they fought as if determined to perpetuate their ancestral renown.

When near San Diego, Kearney's force was surrounded by three or four times its number, and were starving. The men were feeding upon the mules. Even that resource seemed almost exhausted. The utter ruin of the army seemed inevitable. A council of war was held. Carson was present. He was a man of few words. When he spoke, all listened. In his soft, feminine voice he said:

"I think I may be able to creep in the night, through the Mexican lines. I can hasten then to San Diego, and inform Commodore Stockton of our peril. He will hasten to the rescue. I am willing to try."

Immediately Lieutenant Beale, of the United States Navy, one of the most heroic of men, added, "I will go with him." General Kearney accepted the noble offer. In its desperation was his only hope.

The camp was encircled by three concentric rows of sentinels. They were mounted, and rode incessantly to and fro, through their short patrols. Night came. It was dark. Carson and Beale crept out from the camp, on their hands and feet, feeling for the tall grass, the slight depressions in the ground, the shade of the thickets. They had shoes instead of moccasins. As they crept along foot by foot in breathless silence, the stiff soles of the shoes would sometimes hit a stone or a stick, and make a slight noise. They drew off their shoes and pushed them under their belts. Occasionally they were within a few feet of the sentinels, whom they could dimly discern.

They had passed the first line of sentinels, and the second, and were just beginning to breathe a little more freely when a sentinel rode up to within a few feet of the spot where they were lying still as death, and but slightly concealed in the tall grass. By daylight they would have been instantly seen. To their terror the sentinel was mounted, and alighting with flint and steel began to strike a light to indulge in the comfort of his pipe. The flame of a piece of paper would reveal them. The suspense was terrible. So still did they lie and so intense were their inward throbbings that Mr. Carson afterwards affirmed that he could actually hear Lieutenant Beale's heart pulsate.

Providentially the Mexican lighted his pipe, and remounting rode in the other direction. For a distance of nearly two miles Carson and Beale thus crept along, working their way through the Mexican lines. Having left the last sentinel behind them, they regained their feet and felt for their shoes. They were gone. Thus far they had not interchanged even a whisper. Though the worst peril was now over, they had still many dangers to encounter, and fearful suffering. It would not do to advance upon San Diego by any of the well-trodden trails, all of which were closely watched by the enemy's scouts. Carson chose a circuitous route over rocks and hills, where their feet were dreadfully lacerated by the prickly pear.

All the next day, with feet torn and bleeding, they toiled along, feeding upon whatever they could find, which would in the slightest degree appease the gnawings of hunger. Another night spread its gloom around them. Still onward was the march of our heroes. About midnight, Carson discovered, from a slight eminence, the dim outline of the houses in San Diego. They approached the American sentinels, announced themselves as friends, and were conducted to Commodore Stockton. He immediately dispatched one hundred and seventy men with a heavy piece of ordnance, and with directions to march day and night, for the relief of Kearney.

The Mexicans hearing of their approach, knowing

that they would be attacked both in front and rear, fled. Kearney and his army were saved. Carson and Beale had rescued them.

The main army of the Mexicans was now at Los Angelos, about a hundred and twenty miles north from San Diego. They had a strongly intrenched camp there; garrisoned by about seven hundred men. Kearney and Fremont united their forces to attack them. Carson was again with his friend Fremont. The Mexicans were driven away, and the American army took up its winter quarters during two or three cold and dreary months.

In the month of March, 1847, Mr. Carson was directed to carry important dispatches to Washington. Lieutenant Beale, who never recovered from the hardships he encountered in his flight to San Diego, was permitted to accompany him. As we have mentioned, it was a journey of four thousand miles. It was accomplished in three months. In reference to this adventure Mr. Carson writes:

"Lieutenant Beale went with me as bearer of dispatches, intended for the Navy Department. During the first twenty days of our journey he was so weak that I had to lift him on and off his riding animal. I did not think for some time that he could live, but I bestowed as much care and attention on him as any one could have done, under the circumstances. Before the fatiguing and dangerous part of our route was passed over, he had so far recovered as to be able to take care of himself.

" For my attention, which was only my duty to my friend, I was doubly repaid, by the kindness shown to me by his family while I staid in Washington, which was more than I had any reason for expecting, and which will never be forgotten by me."

On this expedition, Kit Carson was provided with a guard of ten or twelve picked men, veteran mountaineers. They took an extremely southern route. Having journeyed about four hundred miles without meeting any hostile encounter, they reached the Gila, a tributary of the lower Colorado. Here Mr. Carson had evidence that a band of hostile Indians, keeping always out of sight, were dogging his path, watching for an opportunity to attack him by surprise. Their route led over a vast prairie, where there were no natural defences. They cooked their supper early in the evening, and wrapped in their blankets, threw themselves on the grass for sleep. Mr. Carson, aware that the cunning Indians might be watching all his movements, as soon as it was dark, ordered his men to rise, march forward in the darkness more than a mile, again to picket their animals, and then to arrange their pack-saddles so as to protect them from the arrows of the Indians. In case of an attack they were to lie perfectly still, and not speak a word. It would be of no use to fire, for no savage would be within sight. If the Indians ventured into the camp, they were then, with rifle, and revolver and knife, to assail them with the utmost desperation.

At midnight the yell of the savage was heard, and a shower of arrows fell around. They had not ascertained with accuracy the position of the travellers. They dared not approach near enough to see, for in that case they could be seen, and the bullet would certainly strike them. After many random shots, and many unearthly yells, the discomfited savages fled. They dared not await the dawn of the day, when upon the open prairie, their arrows would be powerless weapons against rifles. In all these journeyings, Mr. Carson was so cautious that one not acquainted with his well balanced character, might deem him wanting in courage. Not a tree, a rock, a bush, or any other place where an Indian might hide, escaped his notice. His eye was ever scanning the horizon to see if there were any smoke indicating an Indian's fire, or any flight of crows hovering over a spot where Indians had recently encamped. The ground he was ever watching in search of the pressure of the horse's unshod foot, or of the Indian's moccasin.

Colonel Fremont had married the daughter of Missouri's illustrious Senator, Hon. Thomas H. Benton. Mr. Carson, upon his arrival at St. Louis, was taken immediately to Mr. Benton's home, where he was treated with every attention, and where he enjoyed the pleasure of an introduction to the most distinguished men of the city. As in the continuance of his journey he stepped upon the platform of the depot in Washington, Mrs. Fremont was there, with her carriage, to convey him as a guest to her residence.

In the crowd landing from the cars, Mrs. Fremont recognized him at once, from the description which her husband had given. Mr. Carson remained in Washington for several weeks, greatly interested in the entirely new world which was open to him there. His reputation had gone before him, and the very best men in our land honored themselves in honoring Christopher Carson. President Polk appointed him Lieutenant in the United States Rifle Corps. He was then directed to return immediately across the continent as bearer of important dispatches.

Arriving at Fort Leavenworth, in Kansas, he was there furnished with an escort of fifty soldiers to accompany him across the plain. He reached the eastern declivity of the Rocky mountains without important adventure. Here, at a place called Point of Rocks, he overtook a party of United States Volunteers, under command of Lieutenant Mulony. They were escorting a large train of wagons to New Mexico. They encamped not far from each other. Just before the break of day a band of Comanche Indians made an attack upon the cattle of Mulony's party, and got possession of all the oxen and of twenty-six horses.

Mr. Carson, ever on the alert, heard the tumult, and made a sudden and impetuous charge upon the savages. He recovered all the oxen, but the horses were effectually stampeded and lost. But for Mr. Carson, the cattle also would have fallen into the hands of the Indians, which would have been a great calamity. The next day Mr. Carson resumed his rapid march and reached Santa Fe in safety. Here he left his escort in accordance with orders, and hiring sixteen mountaineers, he proceeded on his journey.

Travelling rapidly, he came to Muddy Creek, a tributary of Virgin river. Here he suddenly encountered a camp of three hundred Indians. He knew their reputation as treacherous in the extreme. He threw up a little rampart, forbidding the Indians to draw too near, and then held a parley under the protection of his men. Thoroughly acquainted with the Indian character, he seemed always to know the tone which it was best to assume. Sternly addressing the chiefs, he said:

"I know your treachery. Your words of friendship cannot be believed. Not long ago, you massacred seven Americans. You wish to gain admission to my camp that you may kill us also. I will now allow you till midday to be off. If any of you, after that, are within reach of our rifles you will die."

Most of the Indians were overawed by this bold talk, and disappeared. A few of the more desperate of the warriors lounged about, apparently doubting his words. At the designated hour he ordered his men to take good aim and fire. Though the Indians were at quite a distance, one of the warriors fell instantly dead. Four others were severely wounded. Soon not a savage was to be seen. Thus fifteen men under Carson, vanquished three hundred Indians. "Better," said Napoleon, "is an army of deer led by a lion, than an army of lions led by a deer."

Mr. Carson now pressed on to Monterey, and delivered his dispatches to Colonel Mason. As acting lieutenant in the U. S. army he was placed at the head of a company of dragoons, to guard Tajon Pass, the main outlet through which robber Indian bands conveyed their booty from California to the plains. After spending the winter very successfully in the discharge of this duty, he was again ordered to proceed to Washington with dispatches. Fifteen men were detailed to escort him on the way.

## CHAPTER XIV.

### *The Chivalry of the Wilderness.*

Injustice of the Government.—Heroic Resolve of Mr. Carson.—Indian Outrages.—The valley of Razado.—Barbaric Murders by Apaches.—An Exciting Chase.—An Attractive Picture. Plot of Fox Overthrown.—Gift of Messrs. Brevoort and Weatherhead.—Adventure with the Cheyennes.

ON this second excursion of Mr. Carson to Washington as bearer of dispatches, he learned at Santa Fe, that the Senate of the United States had refused to confirm his appointment as lieutenant. It was a great wrong. Party spirit then ran high at Washington. His friends at Santa Fe advised him to resent the wrong, by delivering his dispatches to the officer in command there, saying he could no longer serve a government which refused to recognize him. His heroic reply was:

"I have been entrusted with these dispatches. I shall try to fulfil the duty thus devolving upon me, if it cost me my life. This is service for my country. It matters little, whether I perform it as lieutenant in the army, or as a mountaineer. I certainly shall not shrink from duty because the Senate does not confirm an appointment which I never sought."

In the then state of the country, there was perhaps not another man who could have conveyed those dispatches over the almost boundless plains, swarming with hostile Indians. It was well known at Santa Fe that the Comanche savages, in bands of two or three hundred, were watching the old Santa Fe road, for two or three hundred miles, that they might murder and rob all who fell into their hands.

Carson resolved to make a trail of his own. He selected but ten men. Pushing directly north, he reached a region which the Comanches seldom visited. Then changing his route, he struck the Bijoux river, and followed it down until within about twenty-five miles of its entrance into the Platte. He then traversed the plains to Fort Kearney, and thence proceeded to Fort Leavenworth without any molestation. His men and animals were in fine condition. His trail, though very circuitous, had led him through a country abounding in game, well watered and with a succession of rich pastures. Here he dismissed his escort, and proceeded to Washington alone.

Having delivered his dispatches, he immediately set out on his return, and reached his home in Taos in October, 1848. He had not been long at home, before the Apache Indians in the vicinity were committing terrible outrages. Colonel Beale, who was in command at Taos, learned that a large party of the savages were upon the upper waters of the Arkansas, with quite a number of white prisoners. He took two companies of dragoons, and Kit Carson as a guide. Upon reaching the river, he found two hundred Indians who had met there in grand council. The force of armed warriors was so strong, and their passions so aroused, that Col. Beale deemed it impossible to liberate the captives, who were Mexicans, by force. He therefore returned to Taos, to resort to the more peaceful operations of diplomacy.

There was at that time residing at Taos, an old mountaineer friend of Kit Carson, by the name of Maxwell, who had become quite rich. Fifty miles east from Taos, there is one of the most lovely valleys in the world called Razado. Fringed with lofty hills of luxuriant foliage, with a mountain stream meandering through the heart of the valley, and with the fertile prairie extending on either side, waving with grass and flowers, a scene is presented which is quite enchanting.

This valley Maxwell and Carson selected for their vast farms, or ranches, as they were called, containing thousands of acres. Maxwell erected a mansion which would be an ornament to any country town. Mr. Carson's dwelling, though more modest, was tasteful, and abounding with comforts. While earnestly engaged in developing and cultivating his farm, he heard that an American merchant by the name of White, while approaching Santa Fe in his private carriage, had been killed by the Apaches, and his wife and only child were carried off by the savages.

A command was immediately organized to pursue the murderers, and rescue the lady if possible. Kit Carson proffered his services for the expedition. The first object was to find the trail. They soon reached the place where the crime had been committed. The ground was strewn with boxes, trunks and pieces of harness, etc., which the savages had not thought it worth while to carry away. They struck the trail and followed it for twelve days without overtaking the fugitives. At last their camp was seen far away in the distance. Kit Carson was the first who caught a glimpse of it. He urged that they should draw unseen as near the camp as possible, and then make a sudden rush upon the Indians, with constant and unerring discharges from their rifles. He said that the savages in their consternation would run, each one to save his own life, without thinking of their captives. If there were a few moments allowed them for thought, they would certainly kill them before effecting their escape.

Unfortunately his counsel was not followed. There was hesitation, delay, and talk of parley. At length they made the attack. The Indians fled before them like deer. The body of Mrs. White was found in the camp, still warm, with an arrow piercing her heart. The savages, on their fresh horses, could not be overtaken by the wearied steeds of the dragoons. They were pursued for six miles. One warrior was killed, and several wounded. Sadly they returned. The little child of Mrs. White had annoyed the Indians by its cries, and with one blow of a tomahawk, its skull had been split open.

Mr. Carson speaking of this adventure modestly writes:

"I am certain that if the Indians had been charged immediately on our arrival, Mrs. White would have been saved. Yet I cannot blame the commanding officer, or the guide, for the action they took in the affair. They evidently did as they thought best; but I have no doubt that they now can see that if my advice had been taken, the life of Mrs. White might have been spared."

The expedition however was not a failure. The Indians were severely punished. Many of them fled with nothing but the scanty clothing they had on.

Mr. Carson returned to Razado. The winter passed peacefully away.

In the spring, a band of Apaches entered the valley, shot the two herdsmen, and drove off a large number of animals. Kit Carson, at the head of ten dragons, set out in sharp pursuit. After a ride of twenty-five miles, they came in sight of them, far away on the prairie. It was an open chase. Soon four of the horses of the dragoons gave out. The remainder of the party, consisting of Carson, six dragoons, and three settlers, pressed on. They soon got near enough to count the numbers of the Indians. There were twenty. Five of them were soon struck by rifle balls, and dropped from their horses. The heroic band returned with the stolen property.

Mr. Carson was now a farmer. In May, 1856, accompanied by an old mountaineer, he took fifty horses and mules to Fort Laramie, a distance of five hundred miles, and sold them to advantage. He then set out for home accompanied only by a Mexican boy. He remained at his farm through the following summer, a peaceful, industrious, busy man, loving his home and enjoying it. He had quite a number of Mexicans employed upon his large farm, whose labors he superintended. Much of his time he employed in hunting, thus abundantly supplying his large family with game. It is written of him, at this time:

"Mounted on a fine horse, with his faithful dog and gun, early each day he would start out on the prairies, to engage in the chase. In a few hours he would return on foot with his noble hunter loaded down with choice game. Sometimes it would be an antelope or elk. On another occasion it would consist of black-tailed deer, which are celebrated as being the largest and finest specimens of venison that roam the forests of any country, and are only to be found in the Rocky mountains; on another, wild turkeys, and then mountain grouse and prairie chickens, helped to complete the load. When thus provided for, it is no wonder that Kit's workmen loved their employment, and labored with good will.

"In his mountain home he was often visited by Indian friends who came to smoke the pipe of peace with him, and to enjoy his hospitality. He saw himself in possession of fine lands, well watered and well timbered. The soil, unsurpassed in richness and fertility, was a safe and sure depository for his seeds, telling him in its silent but unmistakable language, of the harvest in store for him. His stock was the best which heart could wish. And last, but not least, he was within a stone's throw of splendid hunting-grounds."

During the summer two gentlemen, Messrs. Brevoort and Weatherhead, were going to the United States from Santa Fe, with a large sum of money to purchase goods. One of the worst of frontier vagabonds, a fellow by the name of Fox, offered his services as guide, and to organize a company to escort them over the plains. He was a shrewd and plausible scoundrel, and his services were accepted. He enlisted a small but very energetic band of desperadoes, and conspired with them to murder and rob the gentlemen on the way. The deed was to be perpetrated when they should have got nearly across the plains. The murderers could then divide the rich booty among themselves, and scatter throughout the States.

One wretch who had been applied to to join the gang, but who for some unknown reason had declined, divulged the plot when he thought that his friend Fox was so far on his way that there was no danger of his being overtaken and arrested. The rumors of the diabolical plot reached the ears of Kit Carson. He knew Fox and his depraved associates well. The murder was to be perpetrated when the party should reach Cimaron river, about three hundred miles from Santa Fe.

In an hour the energetic man was mounted with a small band of his employés, all upon the fleetest and most powerful steeds. Most of the workmen on Mr. Carson's extended ranche were veteran pioneers. Every man was well armed, and led a horse in addition to the one upon which he rode. It was *possible*, and that was all, that by the most expeditious riding the travellers might be overtaken before the bloody deed had been performed.

Their path was over the open prairie. Onward they went as fast as their steeds could be safely urged. The second night out, they came upon a detachment of United States troops bound for California as recruits. The officer in command, Captain Ewell, knowing that the plains were infested with powerful bands of Indians, by whom the small party of Mr. Carson might be cut off, generously joined him with twenty men, leaving the rest of his party to proceed on their journey by slow marches.

They overtook the merchants just before they had reached the spot where their lives were to be taken. Fox was at once arrested. Messrs. Weatherhead and Brevoort were astounded when informed of the peril from which they had been rescued. Fox was carried back to Santa Fe and placed in jail. The merchants were entrusted to the care of fifteen men who could be relied upon. The rest of the gang were ordered immediately to leave the camp. Though their guilty designs were unquestioned, they would be difficult of proof. The grateful merchants offered Kit Carson a large sum of money for his heroic and successful efforts to save their lives. He replied:

"It is a sufficient reward for me to have been instrumental in saving the lives of two worthy citizens. I can not think of receiving one cent of money."

They all met that night gratefully and joyously, around their camp fires. With the exception of the guilty wretches who had been plotting murder, all were very happy. The emotions excited were too deep to allow of jollity. Indeed Kit Carson was never a jolly man. He had no taste for revelry. As in every man of deep reflection and true greatness, the pensive element predominated in his character.

It was a brilliant night, calm, serene and starlight. As Carson lay awake at midnight, thanking God for what he had been enabled to accomplish, it must have been an hour of sublimity to him, such as is rarely experienced on earth. While most of the numerous party were sleeping soundly around him, nothing could be heard but the howling of packs of prairie wolves, and the heavy tread of the guards, as they walked their beats.

We can not doubt that Mr. Carson was in heart thoroughly a religious man. It is the element of religion alone, which, in the midst of such temptations, could form a character of such remarkable purity. He was too reticent to speak of his own feelings and there were but few, if any, of the thoughtless men around him who could appreciate his christian emotions.

Messrs. Brevoort and Weatherhead made a graceful acknowledgment of their obligations to Mr. Carson for the invaluable service which he had rendered them. In the following spring they presented him with a pair of magnificent revolvers. Upon the silver mountings there was engraved a brief narrative of his heroic achievement. Mr. Carson on his return to Razado, found pleasant and constant employment in carrying on his farm and providing many hungry mouths with game. His hospitable home was ever crowded with guests.

Early in the summer he set out with Mr. Maxwell and a large train of wagons, for the States. Leaving his animals and wagons on the Kansas frontier, he descended the river to St. Louis in a steamboat. Here he purchased a large stock of goods, and reascending the river, transferred them to his caravan. He then started with his long train to return to New Mexico. His route was through the rich pasturage to be found on the way to Bent's Fort. Just before reaching the ford of the Arkansas, he fell in with an encampment of Cheyenne warriors.

They were greatly and justly exasperated by an outrage inflicted upon them by a preceding party of United States recruits. Kit Carson, though unconscious of this, perceived at once that something was wrong. These Indians had been very friendly.

With his customary caution, he ordered the caravan to press forward as rapidly as possible, through the country of the Cheyennes, while every man was ordered to be constantly on guard. Having advanced about twenty miles, he saw that the savage warriors were rapidly gathering around him, in ever increasing numbers. Throwing up an intrenched camp, he rode out to within hailing distance of an advanced party of the warriors, and proposed a council. His friendly words in some degree conciliated them. They were soon seated in a circle, and they smoked the pipe of peace. Carson had addressed them through an interpreter. They did not suppose that the pale face could understand their language. But he did understand it perfectly.

The savages began to talk very loudly among themselves. Carson, understanding every word they said, listened eagerly, hoping to ascertain the cause of their unexpected hostility. Openly, but as they thought secretly, they discussed their plot, treacherously to disarm the whites of their suspicion, and then to arise and massacre them all. With true Indian cunning, they had arranged matters so that it would appear that the Sioux Indians, had perpetrated the massacre, and that the white man's vengeance might fall upon them.

Suddenly Carson sprang to his feet, ordered every man who attended him, to be ready for immediate action. Then to the astonishment of the savages, in pure Cheyenne, he said to them:

"You see that I understand all that you have said. Why do you wish for my scalp? I have ever been the friend of your tribe. No one of you has ever been injured by me. There are some here whom I have met in past years. If they will turn to their memories, they will recall the former hunter of Bent's Fort. I have eaten and drank with them. And now without any provocation from me, you treacherously seek my life. If you do not instantly leave this place, I will order you to be shot."

The warriors disappeared on swift feet. Kit Carson's change of dress had so altered his appearance, that they did not at first recognize him. But they had not forgotten his reputation. Though they had counted his armed teamsters, and saw that they numbered fifteen, the Indian warriors held a grand council, and probably the decision was to withdraw without an attack. Perhaps they remembered their former friendship for Carson; perhaps they were intimidated by his military prowess. At all events, he was not again molested. The remainder of the journey to Razado was accomplished in safety, though the vigilance of this distinguished leader was not intermitted in the slightest degree for a single mile of the way.

## CHAPTER XV.

*Recollections of Mountain Life.*

Character of the Native Indian.—The Caravan.—Interesting Incident. —Effects of Cholera.—Commission of Joe Smith.—Snow on the Mountains.—Government Appointment.—Adventure with three Bears.—Journey to Los Angelos.—Mt St. Bernardino.—The Spring.—Character of Men.—Insubordination Quelled.—Suffering for Water and Relief.—A Talk with Indians.

IN writing the life of Kit Carson, my object has been, as has been mentioned, not merely to record those remarkable traits of character which Mr. Carson developed, but also to portray and perpetuate the great features of that wild and wondrous mountaineer life, which the discovery of this continent ushered in, but even the memory of which is now rapidly passing to oblivion.

It so happens that I have an intimate friend who passed ten years of his early manhood roving through these solitudes. I have spent many an evening hour, listening to his recital of the adventures which he encountered there. This friend, Mr. William E. Goodyear, is a man of unusual native strength of mind, of marvellous powers of memory, and I repose implicit confidence in his veracity. At my earnest solicitation, he has furnished me with the following graphic narrative of the scenes which he witnessed nearly a score of years ago, when these regions were rarely visited save by the wild beast and the Indian.

In the year 1852 I, then a young man, in all the vigor of early youth, and of unusual health and strength, when the wildest adventures were a pleasure, was led by peculiar circumstances to undertake a trip across the continent. Our journey from Independence, Missouri, to Salt Lake was accomplished without any incident worthy of especial record. Along the route we were accompanied by almost an incessant caravan of wagons, horsemen and footmen, some bound to the Mormon city, some flocking to the recently discovered gold mines in California, and some on hunting and trapping excursions, to the vast prairies and majestic valleys of the far west. Here we met several men whose names had attained much renown among the pioneers of the wilderness, such men as James Bridger, Tim Goodell, Jim Beckwith, chief of the Crow Indians, William Rogers, a half breed, and Arkansas Sam

Our company numbered but four, consisting of my uncle, then and now resident in California, who was returning to his home, from a visit to the States;

myself, who was crossing the continent mainly for the love of adventure; another young man, and an Indian boy, about sixteen years old, called Joe. The boy had been brought from the Indian country, and was about as wild and ungovernable a spirit as ever chased a buffalo or shouted the war-whoop.

My uncle had often during the previous twenty years, crossed the mountains, on trapping expeditions with an elder brother. In these adventures my uncle, whom I was accompanying, had become quite familiar with the peculiarities of the Indian, and had become acquainted with many of the chiefs of the different tribes. Neither he nor his brother had even been afraid to enter the camp of the Indian; for they had never deceived nor defrauded him.

Let it be remembered that these excursions of my uncle had taken place nearly forty years ago, before unprincipled traders had carried whiskey into the country and robbed the Indians in every possible way. The native Indian seems to have been the soul of honor. But now how changed! contaminated by vagabond white men.

Our company had about a dozen horses and mules. We rode the horses and the well packed mules carried our luggage. We had also a light two horse spring wagon. Behold us, then, three of us, mounted in half Spanish saddles, with our rifles in front lying crossways between our persons and the horn of the saddle. The never-failing revolver and hunting knife were in our belts. The young man drove the wagon which contained many of our most valuable effects.

It was without much thought that we set out on the emigrant trail to California, a distance of about three thousand miles. As on our journey we were one day descending the hills into the valley of the Platte river, near a place called Ash Hollow, our keen-eyed Indian boy exclaimed, "I see Indians." Looking around with a rapid glance and seeing nothing, I said, "I think not." "Yes," he replied, "there certainly are Indians," and pointed to some specks far away before us, on the meadows which skirted the stream.

Sure enough, there was a band of Indians quite distinctly discernible. My uncle looked at them for a moment quite intently and in silence. Then he said:

"Boys! there is a band of Indians on the war-path. I wish you to obey my instructions exactly. Do not stop your riding animals or the team. Keep straight ahead, unless I tell you to halt. Do not fire a shot unless I fire first. Then take deliberate aim and kill as many as you can before you go under."

"Go under!" this was the almost invariable phrase, in the language of the mountains, for death. I well remember my thoughts as we neared them. It was indeed a formidable looking band of Aripaho Indians, hideously painted, and looking more like demons than men, armed for a fight. They were all mounted, and each warrior carried in his hand a long spear and a strong shield, impervious to arrows, made of rawhide. Their bows and arrows were slung to their backs. To my inexperienced eye they seemed incarnate fiends. We had met several small bands of Indians before, but no war party like this.

When we had approached within a few hundred yards of each other, my uncle said:

"Boys! do not forget what I have told you."

Then pressing his large Mexican spurs into the sides of his horse, he darts away towards them upon the full gallop, at the same time shouting something in the Indian language which I did not understand. Their ranks opened and he rode into the centre and instantly dismounted. There was the chief on a splendid charger. He also alighted, and for a moment both were concealed from our view, buried as it were, within the ranks of the plumed warriors. They were, as we afterwards ascertained, fraternally embracing each other. Both remounted their horses, the ranks opened again and they two, my uncle and the chief, rode out upon the full run towards us as our little cavalcade were steadily pressing forward on the trail.

When they reached us, the chief held out his hand to me, and said in broken English, "How do, brother?" I shook hands with him, returning the salutation of "How do." My uncle then turning to me said, "Have you plenty of tobacco with you?" "O yes," I replied rather tremblingly, for I was ill at ease. "You can have it all if you want it." "I don't want it all," uncle replied. "Give me one plug." I gave it to him and he handed it to the chief.

The war party was directly on the trail. Four hundred mounted warriors occupy much space, composing a formidable looking band. Following the directions which had been given us, we continued on the move. The chief waved a signal to his men, to which they promptly responded, opening their ranks and filing to the right and to the left. We passed on through this living wall bristling with spears, meeting with an occasional greeting of "How do." Having passed through the long lines of the band my uncle said to me, "Keep straight on till night. I will then rejoin you. I am going to have a big smoke with the chief."

With alacrity we obeyed this mandate, glad enough to leave such customers behind us. I confess that I was half frightened to death, and feared I should never see my uncle again. In the evening he joined us and laughed very heartily at me for wishing, in my trepidation, to give the chief all my tobacco.

In after life, in my intercourse with the Indians, I got bravely over being scared by any sights or sounds emanating from them. We pressed on without molestation to Salt Lake, passing continually the newly made graves of the dead. The cholera had broken out with awful fatality, along the whole line of the emigrants' march, consigning thousands to burial in the wilderness.

We reached the Great Salt Lake, the home of the Mormons, in safety. Here we remained for nearly a month. I called on Brigham Young, and also on the old patriarch Joe Smith. From the latter I received a commisson, or power of attorney, for the consideration of two dollars, authorizing me to heal the sick, to raise the dead, and to speak all languages. Perhaps my want of faith left me as powerless as other men, notwithstanding my commission. We spent our time here in strolling around the city, visiting the tabernacle, bathing and fishing in the river Jordan, which empties into the lake, and in making sundry purchases for the continuation of our journey to the Pacific.

Again we started upon our journey. After weary days of travel, without encountering any adventure of special interest, we reached the vast ridge of the Sierra Nevada mountains. Up, up, and still up, the trail led us over the gigantic cliffs. On the summit we found snow hundreds of feet deep, and apparently as hard as the rock which it surmounted. We crossed the ridge by what is called the Carson route. Descending the mountains on the western side, we find ourselves in California, and pressing on through Sacramento, to Benicia, are at our journey's end.

We left Independence on the third of June. It is now the latter part of September. We have spent almost four months on the road. And here let me say, that had I given a description of the country, its rivers, its mountains, its scenery, its abundance of game, among the noblest of which, are the buffalo, bears of different kinds, deer, antelope, mountain sheep; its numerous rivers abounding with a great variety of fishes,—had I endeavored to give a full description of all these, it would have demanded a volume rather than a chapter.

Here I was at Benicia, and winter was at hand. I decided not to go to the mining districts until the spring sun should return. Provisions commanded almost fabulous prices. Packers got a dollar a pound for packing flour, sugar, rice and other things which the miners must have.

But an unexpected opening presented itself to me. Mr. Frederick Loring was about to set out on a surveying tour in behalf of the government. I secured a position in the party as chain-man.

We set out for San Rafael, which is in Marin county, on the coast of the Pacific, just north of San Francisco. We had been out but five or six weeks, when Mr. Loring's health began seriously to fail him. One day he called me to him, and said:

"I wish you now to quit chaining and to carry my instrument and to watch me, that you may learn to use it yourself. I shall probably not be able to finish this contract. I ought to be on my bed now."

Very readily I fell in with this arrangement. Having studied navigation while a boy at school, which is somewhat similar to surveying, it did not take me a great while to learn to adjust the instrument, or to take the variations at night, on the elongation of the north star. I will here remark in passing, that Mr. Loring soon became so enfeebled that he returned to San Francisco, where he died.

One day while surveying in the coast range, we had descended a mountain, and upon a plain below had found a dense chaparral or thicket of bushes, so closely interwoven that we could not penetrate it with our pack animals. We therefore sent the boys down the plain, along the edge of the thickets, to find some better place to go through. Mr. Loring, our chain-man and I prepared to make a triangulation, in order to get the distance from the point we were at, to a white stone on our line of survey, which was on the side of the opposite mountain and across the chaparral.

Having finished the triangulation, Mr. Loring and I endeavored to cross the chaparral by a direction different from that which the main body of the party was pursuing. Suddenly Mr. Loring dropped his instrument and in a tone of terror exclaimed:

"Look at that bear." I looked as he pointed in the direction of a large rock, and there were three huge grizzly bears. Loring, being longer legged than I, left me like a shot from a gun. I ran to a tree, near by, from four to six feet in circumference, and very speedily found myself perched among its branches. I looked for the bears. One had not left the spot where we discovered them. Another was growling and snarling at the foot of the tree which I had climbed. The other was going after Loring at no very slow pace.

We had got through the chaparral and our party

with the mules had also come across and were many rods farther down the valley, coming up to meet us. As Loring fled with the speed of an antelope, he met the first animal, which happened to be the kitchen mule. He was so called, because he had very large open bags or panniers, into which we put all our cooking utensils. Loring sprang upon the back of the mule. At the same moment the animal caught sight of the grizzly bear. Frantic with terror, he turned and fled as mule never fled before. Down went the mule on the back track along the edge of the chaparral. Once in a while, as the bags flew around, they would catch on the bushes, and tear a hole. Soon the tin cups and plates began to fly, the mule kicking at them with every jump, making such a din as to set all the rest of the animals flying through the bushes, and down the trail in the wildest imaginable stampede. The huge bear in mad pursuit was rushing after them.

It was a sight I shall never forget. Loring on the cook's mule hanging on with all his might. The tin ware flying in all directions. All the boys as well as your humble servant, up in the trees looking on. I laughed so heartily at the ludicrous scene, that I was in danger of falling, in which case the bear would have torn me to pieces right quick.

But who is this coming towards me? He is an

old hunter of our party who used to make shingles in the Red-woods. He has had two sons killed by bears. Now he has joined our party to provide us with game. Deliberately, he walks up to within ten feet of the bear who is growling at the foot of my tree. Bruin turns on his new foe, and rising on his hind feet, with appalling howlings, prepares for battle. But in an instant the old man's rifle is at his shoulder. His eye runs quickly through the sights, an explosion follows, and the bear is dead. The hunter knew well where to strike a vital point. Satisfied that the monster was powerless, I came down from the tree.

The other bear, apparently dismayed by the commotion he had created, turned into the chaparral and disappeared. It required all the rest of the day to re-collect our party and to repair damages.

Let us now pass from these scenes to the spring of the year 1854. Here we are then in San Francisco, all ready to start on board the Sea Bird. "Cast off the lines." "Aye, aye, sir." Off we go around North Beach. You will see Point Boneta on the north, and Point de los Lobos on the south. Through the straits we go out at the Golden Gate. Onward we glide past Farallones de los Frayles, and here we are out on the broad Pacific.

After sailing about three hundred miles south we

arrive at San Pedro. We go ashore at once and secure seats in the stage for Ciudad de los Angelos, which is situated about twenty-five miles from here in a northerly direction. There is now, after the lapse of twenty years, a railroad, instead of Banning's stages, by which one can be transported to the City of Angels. We shall be obliged to stay here for a few days, to prepare our outfit. Let us see what we want. Mules and jacks, pack-saddles, saddles for ourselves to ride, in fact every thing pertaining to camp-life. Here we can get almost any thing we wish for man or beast.

Well then we will suppose that now we are ready to start. Away we go towards San Bernardino. We pass the finest of vineyards where thousands of gallons of wine are made. On, on we go, and at last, after a ride of about seventy miles, we arrive at San Bernardino. One of the first things which attracts our attention is the mountain of the same name. It rises seventeen thousand feet above the level of the ocean, attaining an altitude two thousand feet above that of Mont Blanc, the monarch of the Alps.

The inhabitants of the towns are, with few exceptions, Mormons. It was from this place that we started on a survey, commencing east of the coast range of mountains, and extending our operations to the extreme boundary line of California, on the east,

The Colorado river was then the line which separated California from New Mexico.

The party employed in this surveying tour consisted of about forty men. The first day we went as far as the mouth of the Cahon Pass, by which we were to penetrate through the coast range of which I have spoken. At this spot we found a large farm, which they call a ranche, where provisions can be purchased, and also poor whiskey. We rested here for the night, sleeping in the open air, and at an early hour in the morning, sprung from our blankets ready dressed. The cook speedily prepared our breakfast, we ate like hungry men and then packed our mules and jacks, and were on our way. Our pack animals will carry from two to three hundred pounds without any trouble.

Nearly at the eastern end of the pass we came to water. This I claim that I discovered, or at least that my horse discovered it for me. It is called in Spanish *Guilliome Bobo*, or "William I Drink." No one would see the spring unless narrowly looking for it. It trickles down the almost perpendicular side of the mountain. We encamped at the spring, and in the morning made an early start, as we had some forty or fifty miles to go that day. But we had a serious job to encounter before we could get out of this defile. It is so steep at its eastern extremity, that we had to unpack and send up very small loads at a time. In some places we had to use ropes, to haul up our goods.

But after a while everything is ready for another start. On, on we go, through a barren cactus country, till we reach the Mohavè river. The day is far spent, we are all very weary, men as well as animals. So, boys, off with the packs of provisions, and let your mules go with their long hair ropes. Let one of the men be sent to look out for the animals. This was no sooner said than done. I was captain of my men. A harder set could not be found, in any prison in this or any other land.

My lieutenant, whose name was Texas, had but one eye and he was covered with scars. But notwithstanding the company was a hard one, it was the best I could get for my use. Almost all of them had been in many a fight. Before they had been with me three months, I have reason to believe every one of them loved me, and I know that they feared me. Only two instances of mutiny occurred in over two years and a half. Both of these I will here relate.

On one occasion I observed that some of the jacks had been kicked severely. I said to my packmaster, "Mr. Williams, how is this? Those jacks have been shamefully used. The skin is off and the wounds are bleeding. I, as you well know, hold you personally responsible for every animal. Don't let me ever see this again, sir."

As I turned to go from him, I heard him mutter something. I at once, with my hand upon my revolver, came back towards him and inquired, "what's this you're saying, sir?"

He replied, "I kicked the jacks myself and I will do it again if they bother me."

I walked to within perhaps ten paces of him and said, "If I ever catch you at it, I will shoot you like a dog."

"Two," he replied, "can play at that game," and his hand neared the butt of his revolver. I jerked out my pistol and fired at his arm. His pistol dropped to the ground.

"Don't shoot again, captain. I will do as you wish in the future."

"All right," said I. "Let me see your arm."

I had shot him through his wrist. I bound up the wound as well as I could, and it soon healed. He remained in my employ nearly four years after that, and to my knowledge was never guilty of doing me or my animals a wrong.

Another instance happened a long time after this. I was getting short of provisions, and had got to do just so much work within a certain time. So I resolved to run two instruments. As we were then running sectional lines, I could take the variations at night. So I fixed another instrument and gave it into the hands of a young man by the name of Biddleman. I assigned to him his part of the line then, and set him at work within three miles of the camp.

Returning to camp about two o'clock in the afternoon, to do some traverse work around a small lake, what was my astonishment, to see that Biddleman's party was already in camp. Upon asking him what it meant, he told me that upon running a random line, he stopped to correct the error at the half mile corner, and that his men on getting to the mile corner, instead of coming back and reporting the error as they should have done, started for camp. He, of course, followed on, as he could not do anything alone.

at once called his party of men, told them to get their chain and pins, put the stakes, pickaxe and shovel on the line animal, and follow me. This they did. When we got to the corner where Biddleman left off work, I set my instrument, gave them an object to run by, and sent them off. They went and returned to me. I then ran another mile north, set my instrument and started them east again on random. They went and I followed them to the half mile corner, to which place they returned

I said: "Boys, we will now go to camp. In future whether with me or Biddleman, you will continue at your work until you are directed to return."

Had I allowed either of the above transactions to have passed unpunished, I might as well have started for the States, for all order would have been at an end.

Sometimes we would see a small party of Indians at a short distance from us. I would step to my instrument, and turn the glass towards them. They would at once commence to scamper, throw sand, turn into all manner of shapes, lie down, roll over, thinking no doubt it was a gun or something that would destroy them. At one time, I attempted to cross from the sink of the Mohavè river to Providence, some sixty miles, expecting to find water at Washburn's well. This was a hole which I afterwards found dug down about ten feet in the white sand that covers this desert. On this sand not any thing grows, but musquit bush, which bears a bean that the Indians eat.

After travelling to within twelve miles of the mountain, my animals and my men all gave out. We did not have a drop of water, and my chart said that there was none short of the mountain. I told the boys that evening was coming on, and I would take some leather bottles we had and go and get some water as quickly as I could. So just before dark, I started with bottles enough to hold twenty quarts. I had a trail to follow in the dark, not over a foot in width. After what seemed to me the longest twelve miles I ever travelled, I arrived at the mountain. After following the ravine through the top, I found the spring, drank heartily, filled my bottles, and started on my return trip. I arrived at the place where I had left my men, just as the day was breaking. After giving them a good drink, I gave some to each of the animals, any one of which would drink from a canteen or bottle.

We then all immediately started on towards the mountain, at which place we finally arrived. When within about fifty yards of the spring, I saw a small party of Indians camped just above it. One of them, the chief, stepped forward, and in Spanish ordered me to stop. And here let me say, that almost all of the Indians, especially their chiefs, can talk Spanish. When he ordered me to stop, I burst out into a laugh, and asked him "what for." My boys in the meantime were preparing for a fight. I told them to put up their weapons, as I did not wish to commence fighting the Indians here, as there were lots of them, and we had a good deal of work to do in that vicinity. Though we might kill or capture all of this party, a larger band might attack us in the future. So I told the boys that if they would keep still, I would bother the Indians a little, and then let them go. This was agreed to. Upon my asking the chief *what for*, he said,

"This water belongs to the Indians."

I replied, "Do you call yourselves Indians? You are nothing but squaws and papooses. I was here last night, and got water under your very noses, and you did not know it."

"The white captain," the chief replied, "talks with two tongues. He lies."

"You are the one that lies," I rejoined. "Has the chief lost his eyesight? Is he so old that he cannot see the white man's trail? Let him come forward and meet his white brother alone, and he will show him his trail."

He at once advanced as I did myself. We shook hands. I pointed out my last night's trail. He saw it at once, and turning to his companions, said to them,

"The white captain has told the truth."

So we shook hands all around. I gave them some hard bread, also some bacon, and we had a good time generally all day resting at this spring. At nightfall they all departed, as silently as shadows, leaving us in full possession of the spring of water.

## CHAPTER XVI.

*Recollections of Mountain Life.*

Position of The Spring.—The Cachè.—Kit Carson's Character and Appearance.—Cool Bravery of a Mountain Trapper.—Untamed Character of Many Hunters.—The Surveyor's Camp in an Indian Territory.—Terrors from Indians.—Joe Walker.—A Mountain Man.—Soda Lake.—Optical Illusion.—Camp on Beaver Lake.—The Piyute Chief. Conversation with Him.—An alarm.—A Battle.

MR. GOODYEAR in his interesting narrative continues: Here let me speak a word or two about water. The springs, as a general thing, are found near the summit of the mountains. In some cases I have had to pack the water a distance of forty miles, for months at a time. From a lake where it bubbled up from the bottom as warm as you would like to hold your hand in, the process of evaporation in the leather bottles rendered it soon, almost as cool as ice water.

Let us now return to our first camping-ground on the Mohavè river. Here I *cached* or buried for concealment, some of my provisions, to relieve the animals of their heavy load. If Mr. Indian does not find the *cache*, it will be all right on our return. I will explain how we do it. First, then, we send out two or three men as scouts, to see if they can discover any signs of Indians, such as footprints or trail, or smoke, or anything of that kind. Men that are used to it, can distinguish between the footprints of an Indian and a white man. They can also, at a long distance off, tell an Indian fire from a white man's.

Any mountaineer can tell by the trail, how long since persons have passed, the number of the party, as well as the number of animals. An Indian, when he makes a fire, uses half a dozen little sticks as big as your thumb, and very dry, and all the smoke the fire makes, will ascend straight up in one steady column. The white man will use, if he is a novice, the dry to kindle with, and then he will chuck on the wet wood, which will cause a great smoke.

But to return to my *cache*. I keep out my scouts all the time we are to work. "Boys, get your shovels, and dig a hole about four or five feet deep, by ten feet in length. Put a lot of wood or branches in the bottom. In with the provisions, canvas over the top, or more bushes. Cover over all with earth. Then take ashes from previous fires, and scatter over the top; then build fires over them, so as to dry the sand.

It was here in this camp that I first met Christopher Carson, or Kit Carson, as he was called. From his wide acquaintance with the Indians on both sides of the Rocky mountains; from his personal knowledge of the many tribes of the red men; from his bravery under all circumstances in which he has been placed, Kit Carson stands at the head of all the hardy pioneers of the Great West. It is now more than twenty years, since I first met him on the Mohavè river, about eighty miles from San Bernardino.

He was accompanied by an American and half a dozen Mexicans or half breeds, who were assisting him to drive some sheep. As he rode up, he saluted me with Buenos dias Señor, which means 'good day sir.' I answered the salutation in the same language, at the same time clasping his hand as he dismounted, and introduced himself as Kit Carson. He is about five feet eight or nine inches high, and weighs about one hundred and sixty pounds. He had a round, jolly looking face, a dark piercing eye, that looked right through you, and seemed to read your every thought. His long brown hair hung around his shoulders. His dress consisted of buckskin coat and pants, with leggins coming up to his knees, and in which he carried, in true Mexican style, his Machete or long two-edged knife.

His coat and pants were heavily fringed, in which the quills of the porcupine bore a conspicuous part. A cap of fox-skin surmounted his head, with four coon's tails sticking out around the edges of the cap. On his feet were moccasins. His never-failing rifle was strapped to his back, as also a powder-horn and bullet-pouch, which latter contained bullets, lead and moulds. Around his waist there was a heavy belt, which was fastened by a large, highly polished silver buckle. Attached to the belt, were a pair of revolvers and a hunting knife.

The noble steed by which he stood, was gayly caparisoned, in true Mexican style. In many places his trappings were covered with gold and silver. His bridle also glittered with silver ornaments and buckles.

Thus Kit Carson stands before you, the beau ideal of a mountain man, or trapper, always ready to help every one in distress, or to avenge an injury, and no matter what the odds, would fight to the death, believing that if he went under, fighting for his friends, it was all right.

Kit Carson was a host in himself. It is my belief that he was feared, singly and alone, more than any other trapper in the Indian country. For my own part, in an Indian fight, many a one of which I have been in, I would rather have Carson than twenty common men. His name struck terror to an Indian. And if it were known that Kit, with a companion or two, was on their trail, they would flee faster than they would from a whole regiment of Uncle Sam's men. If Kit was after them, they might as well commence their death song at once, and prepare for their happy hunting grounds, for he would surely catch them any where this side of that.

But I must not forget the names of other brave trappers, with whom I became acquainted, and who often shared with me my camp in the Indian country, such as Peg Leg Smith, Joseph Walker, and a host of other brave men. I will here tell you how Smith got his name of Peg Leg.

Thirty years ago, he and some of his companions were trapping in the Indian country. They had made a hut in a ravine. For a camping place, it was so well concealed, that for a long time they were undisturbed. One day, however, Smith and three or four of his party were discovered by Indians, about two miles from camp. A fight took place, in which Smith was struck by a rifle ball, that shattered the bone below the knee. He fell, and during the melee managed to crawl into a thicket, unobserved either by the Indians or his own men. Here, after tying up his own leg with buckskin thongs which he cut from his hunting shirt, he very coolly and deliberately went to work with his own knife, and cut his own leg off. After this he crawled to his camp, where he found his companions who supposed he was dead, and who were expecting the next morning to go and find his body.

This is said to be a true story, and who of thoes who were in California twenty years ago, do not remember Peg Leg Smith and his horse John. He would come into San Francisco, or Benicia, riding like the wind, his long grey hair floating about his shoulders, and then that never-to-be-forgotten war-whoop! And now here in Benicia, he dashes up to the Vallejos hotel.

"John," he says to his horse, "down sir, quick. I'm mighty dry." Down goes the horse; old Peg gets off. "Boys, how are you. I say there," addressing the bar tender, "make me a whiskey toddy."

This is done at once. No pay is expected. No one expects Peg Leg Smith to pay for any thing, where he is known.

Most of these men possessed many noble impulses, and would prove true to the death for their friends. But they considered the killing of an Indian as justifiable, whenever they met with one.

I was at this time at work under Colonel Jack Hayes, of Texas. Every one familiar with the history of that State in its infancy, will remember him as an old Indian fighter. He was one who never turned his back on friend or foe. At this time, he was United States Surveyor-General of California.

Some may like to know how we camp in an Indian country. I will give a brief description of our camp. First our pack saddles are placed in a circle, enclosing a pretty large space. Our provisions and goods are then stored inside of the circle. Our animals are picketed at our heads, the pack saddles serving as pillows, and our feet being towards the centre of the circle. When there is danger to be apprehended, the animals are placed within the circle. But ordinarily, they graze to the extent of their picket ropes upon the rich grass outside. Generally inside the circle there is a rousing fire. Those of us who are not on guard, lie down in our blankets, feet towards the fire. Our rifles are placed in the hollow of the left arm; our revolvers at our back. ready for instant use. The sky is our covering, the earth our support. The guard patrols on the outside the circle, outside the horses. We go to sleep to dream of home and friends, and often to be awakened by the quick sharp bark of the cayote, the howling of the grey wolf, or what is far worse, the almost infernal war-whoop of the Indian.

My orders to each man, in case of an attack, were not to rise. The guard also, as they came inside the circle of pack saddles, were to throw themselves flat on the ground. Those that were in their blankets were to roll over on their stomachs, and then when they saw an Indian to 'blaze away.' When we were on the line and expected trouble, we would build a fire and at dark, after supper, move away slowly for one or two miles, and lie down without any fires, and in this way cheat Mr. Indian.

Sometimes after working all day we were obliged to fight for our lives all the latter part of the night; for this is the time which the Indian chooses for his fighting, as a general rule. Notwithstanding these apparent drawbacks, I must say that the life of a mountain man or trapper, had ever indescribable charms for me.

And now in conclusion, let me give you an account of my last Indian fight, which happened in the year 1859, on the Colorado river, near what is now called Fort Mohavè. At that time the Indians in that region had seen but few white men, and they had obtained but about half a dozen old guns. I, having surveyed a large portion of the country previously, was chosen to act as guide to Colonel Hoffman, who was to be escorted by fifty dragoons from Fort Tejou, near Los Angelos, to Fort Yuma. I, not then being acquainted with the country upon the Colorado river down to the fort, the celebrated scout and trapper Joe Walker, was to go with us, to act as guide after we had passed through that portion of the country with which I was acquainted.

Joe was a tall, large man, six feet high and weighing over two hundred pounds. We slept together in the same blankets, and many a night have I laid awake, listening to his stories of fights with the Indians and his hair-breadth escapes.

I shall pass rapidly over our journey across the mountains and along the valley of the Mohavè river. Away we go across Soda Lake, which is dry, and the surface of which as far northward as the eye can extend, is covered with saleratus, white as the driven snow. If you should see at a distance anything coming towards you, it would seem to approach bottom upwards; if an animal, the feet would be in the air.

But on we go to the Granite springs, thence we pass on to Piyute Creek. Slowly we ascend the mountains from which we are to descend to the Colorado river. Colonel Hoffman orders a halt, for the smoke of Indian fires is seen ascending for miles along the banks of the majestic river. Having got all things prepared for either peace or war, we march down into the valley. The Indians have undoubtedly caught sight of us, for suddenly the smoke disappears, all the fires apparently being extinguished. We press on and soon reach the banks of the river.

Following down the stream a mile or two, the colonel searches for a good spot for a camping-ground. As we are on the move, all mounted, well armed and in military array, about thirty Indians showed themselves. Moving cautiously at first, they gradually became emboldened and ran along our lines asking sundry questions. But we returned no answers. Having selected the spot for camping-ground, we lay out our camp in the form of a triangle. On the one side is a bluff from six to ten feet high, on the opposite side is a lake called Beaver Lake, about five hundred yards wide. Here, upon the rich grass which borders the lake, we tether our animals, each one having the range of a rope about thirty feet long. Here we considered them safe, as the Indians would hardly attempt to attack them. It was early in the month of January, 1859.

The third side of our triangle was a dry swamp, covered with a dense growth of willow bushes. By order of the colonel, these bushes were cut down for a distance of sixty or eighty yards, so that no foe could approach unseen. By four o'clock in the afternoon, the labor of establishing our camp was completed. At some distance from us there was a large and constantly increasing band of Indians, curiously watching our proceedings. They weie all well armed with their native weapons of lances, bows and arrows.

As I was talking in one part of the camp with Joe Walker, Colonel Hoffman approached us and said,

"I want one of you to go and have a talk with the Indians."

"Very well sir," I replied, and turning to Joe, added, "will you go, or shall I?"

"You had better go, I guess," Joe replied.

I at once set out towards the Indians, and when I arrived within speaking distance, hailed them in Spanish, saying that I wished to see their chief and to have a talk. I had left my rifle in the camp, but still had my revolvers, and my knife. A young fellow, tall, of splendid proportions, and one of the fiercest looking Indians I ever saw, stepped out towards me, with his bows and arrows. He was entirely naked except his breach clout and a small plaid shawl thrown over his shoulders. The ends were fastened down by a piece of black tape. On this tape was strung a pair of common shears, apparently as an ornament.

His color was like a new piece of copper, clear, brilliant and exceedingly beautiful, like one of the most majestic statues in shining bronze. "How do you do?" said he, in Spanish, as he approached me and held out his hand. I took his hand, returning the salutation in the same language.

"Why do you come here?" he then promptly said. "This is our country. We have nothing to give you, for yourselves or your horses."

I gave him some tobacco in token of good will, and then replied: "We have come to look at the country. We do not wish you to give us anything. If you are friendly, we shall give you presents. If you attack us, we shall kill you." I then added: "Some of the Indians of this country massacred a party only a year ago. We shall have no more killed by them. We shall build a fort here, to protect our emigrants."

He replied a little angrily, "I am a Mohavè. My people own this country. I shall kill whoever I please." I had not any doubt that the shawl and the shears came from the party they had massacred. I pointed to the shawl and said:

"Where did you get that?"

"I bought them," he replied, evidently annoyed. "I bought them from the Piute Indians."

"My brother," I replied, "does not talk with a straight tongue. It is forked, and his words are crooked." He now added, with considerable warmth:

"Go to your own camp, and prepare for war. I

will not kill you. Your guns are short. I will take your horses, and my men shall have a big feast Your horses are fat and good. I have many men many braves. You have but few. Go to your camp and prepare for war."

"Indian," said I, "I go, but remember that our short guns kill an Indian every time. We never stop to load them."

I turned to go back to the camp. It is not etiquette on such an occasion to back out, watching your opponent, as though you were a coward and feared an attack. I turned squarely round, with my back to the Indian, when I saw the boys at the fort suddenly raise their rifles with their muzzles directed towards us. At that moment, an arrow whizzed through my buckskin shirt, just making a flesh wound on the shoulder. I had slightly turned as the arrow left the bow, otherwise I should probably have received my death-wound. Instantly, with my revolver already in my hand, I discharged in quick succession, two shots at the savage, who was distant but a few feet from me. The first bullet broke his arm; the second passed through his heart. I instantly seized the shawl and shears and taking a little of his hair to remember him by, started on a jump towards our men, who were rushing towards me as fast as possible. The arrows flew so thick and fast, that you would have thought it was hailing. Night soon came on, and the Indians retired, probably to get recruits and to renew the battle in the morning with the certainty of our destruction. We doubled our guard for the night, during which I was awakened but once. Joe Walker and I slept together. So much used were we both to such little affairs, that I do not believe we should have awakened at all, had we not been called.

About twelve o'clock, a sentry came to where we were sleeping, and touching me, said:

"Guide, I believe there is an Indian creeping up behind a bush." Joe says, "Bill, get up and see what it is. My eyes are not as good in the night as yours."

So out of my blanket I got, grabbed my revolver and went towards the bluff. The sentinel accompanying me, pointed out the bush. I did not like to fire into it, lest I should give a false alarm. I watched it about ten minutes, and there was not the least movement. "I guess," I said, "it is nothing but a bush." But at that moment, I perceived a very slight agitation of the branches. It proved that there must be somebody there.

"Oho! Mr. Indian," I exclaimed, "at your old tricks. I raised my revolver, took deliberate aim at the very heart of the bush, and fired. Mr. Indian gave a hideous yell, and he had gone to his happy hunting grounds. In the morning, we prepared to leave. The Indians, as we afterwards learned, had fifteen hundred warriors within a radius of five miles. We numbered but about fifty men. But we had rifles, they had only bows and arrows. The superiority of our arms raised us above all fear.

It was manifest however, with the earliest dawn, from the large number of warriors assembled, and the menacing cries they raised, that we must have a fight. Colonel Hoffman detached every fourth man, each one to hold four horses. The rest of the dragoons were marshalled on the bluff, which as I have mentioned, lined one side of our encampment. As our rifles could throw a bullet more than twice as far as any arrow could be thrown, the battle was rather a source of amusement to us, than of terror. No Indian could approach within arrow shot of our ranks, without meeting certain death. It must be confessed that we had no more compunctions in shooting an Indian than in shooting a bear or a wolf. As they dodged from tree to tree, assailing us with their impotent arrows, our keen marksmen watched their opportunity to strike them down with the invisible death-dealing bullet.

Old Joe Walker practiced with our Hawkins' rifles and revolvers, as he said, "just to keep his hand in." After an hour or two of this strange battle, in which the Indians suffered fearful carnage, and we encountered no loss, our foe in rage and despair retired. They left sixty of their number dead, besides taking with them many wounded. We continued our march without further molestation.

And now my friend, if you shall find anything interesting to you in this short sketch, I shall be satisfied. I have written a great deal more than I expected to write, when I began. And yet you have but a very brief narrative of my adventures in California.

Yours truly,

(signed) WILLIAM E. GOODYEAR.

## CHAPTER XVII.

*Frontier Desperadoes and Savage Ferocity.*

Original Friendliness of the Indians.—The River Pirates, Culbert and Magilbray.—Capture of Beausoliel.—His Rescue by the Negro Cacasotte.—The Cave in the Rock.—The Robber Mason.—His Assassination.—Fate of the Assassins.—Hostility of the Apaches. Expedition of Lieutenant Davidson.—Carson's Testimony in his Favor.—Flight of the Apaches.

WE have occasionally alluded to the desperadoes who infested the frontiers. They were often much more to be dreaded than the Indians. Indeed the atrocities which these men perpetrated were the main cause of the hostility of the savages. It is the uncontradicted testimony that the natives were, at first, disposed to be friendly. It was only when exasperated by unendurable wrongs that they appealed to arms. When seemingly unprovoked assailants, they were seeking revenge for some great outrage which they had already experienced, from the depraved vagabonds of the wilderness.

When St. Louis was under Spanish rule, there had sprung up quite a brisk commerce between that settlement and New Orleans. But the shores of the majestic Mississippi were then infested by large bands of robbers, watching to attack and plunder boats, as they ascended and descended the stream. There were two leaders of one of these large bands, by the name of Culbert and Magilbray, who, occupying commanding points, were carrying on a regular system of river piracy.

In the year 1739, a merchant by the name of Beausoliel, had sailed from New Orleans, in a barge richly freighted with goods, bound for St. Louis. The robbers, pushing out from the shore in their light canoes, and well armed, captured the boat without a struggle. They ordered the owner and the crew into the little cabin and fastened them in.

There was a negro on board, a very remarkable man, by the name of Cacasotte. Though carved in ebony, he had great beauty of countenance, and wonderful grace and strength of person. His native, mental endowments were also of a high order. This man, Cacasotte, as soon as the barge was taken, assumed to be greatly overjoyed. He danced, sang and laughed, declaring that he would no longer live in irksome slavery, but that he would join the band, and enjoy liberty among the freebooters as their attendant.

He was so jovial, and so attentive, in anticipating a'l their wants, that he won their confidence, and they all thought that he would be a valuable addition to their company. He was thus permitted to roam over the boat, unmolested and unwatched. He formed a plan in all its details, for the recapture of the boat, and the liberation of the crew. This plan he succeeded in communicating to his master. Mr. Beausoliel had his earthly all in the boat, and he also expected that the pirates would take their lives. He was therefore ready to adopt any plan, however desperate, which gave any promise of success. We have the following account given in "The Great West," of the plan the negro formed and of its successful accomplishment.

"Cacasotte was cook, and it was agreed, between him and his fellow conspirators, likewise too negroes, that the signal for dinner should also be the signal for action. When the hour arrived, the robbers assembled in considerable numbers on the deck, and stationed themselves on the bow and stern and along the sides, to prevent any rising of the men. Cacasotte went among them with the most unconcerned demeanor imaginable. As soon as his comrades had taken their assigned stations he placed himself at the bow, near one of the robbers, a stout herculean fellow, who was armed cap-à-pie. Cacasotte gave the preconcerted signal, and immediately the robber near him was struggling in the water.

With the speed of lightning he ran from one robber to another, as they were sitting on the sides of the boat and, in a few seconds' time, had thrown several of them overboard. Then seizing an oar he struck on the head those who had attempted to save themselves by grappling the running boards. He then shot with rifles, which had been dropped on deck, those who attempted to swim away. In the meantime his companions had done almost as much execution as their leader."

Thus every one of these robbers found a watery grave. Mr. Beausoleil had his property restored to him, and pressing all sail went on his way rejoicing.

A few years after this, about the year 1800, there was a noted robber named Mason, who occupied what is called, "The Cave in the Rock." This renowned cavern was about twenty miles below the Wabash river. Its entrance was but a few feet above high water-mark, and opened into a very remarkable chamber, two hundred feet long, eighty feet wide and twenty-five feet high. Throughout the whole central length the floor was quite level, and on each side of this central aisle the sides rose in tiers, like the seats of an amphitheatre.

This remarkable cave is connected with another a little above. Here this Mason, a man of gigantic stature, and of inferior education and intellect, had his concealed retreat, with two sons and several other desperadoes, organized into a band of land and water pirates. With great skill they prosecuted their robberies, plundering boats as they descended the river, but more often watching the return boats, to rob the owners of the money which they had received from the sale of their cargoes.

As the population of the Ohio valley increased, Mason deemed it expedient to abandon the Cave in the Rock and established himself with his gang, on a well known and much frequented trail called the Nashville and the Natches Trace. Here his gang became the terror of the whole travelling community. Sometimes, with his whole band decorated in the most gaudy style of Indian warriors, with painted faces, and making the forest resound with hideous yells, they would swoop down upon a band of travellers, inflicting outrages which savages could not exceed.

The atrocities of which this desperate gang were guilty, at length became so frequent and daring, accompanied with the most brutal murders, that Governor Claiborne, of the Mississippi Territory, offered a large reward for the capture of Mason dead or alive. But the wilderness of prairie, forest and mountain was very wide. Mason was familiar with all its lurking places. For a long time he baffled all the efforts of the authorities for his capture.

Treachery at last delivered him to the hands of justice, or rather brought his ignominious career to a close, inflicting upon him the violent and bloody death which he had so often inflicted upon peaceful and innocent merchants and travellers. Two of his own band, tempted by the large reward which was offered, and perhaps maddened by his tyranny, for he ruled his gang with a rod of iron, conspired to kill him. They watched their opportunity and one day, as Mason was counting out the money he had just gained by the robbery of some merchants, one of them advancing from behind him, struck a hatchet into his brain. The accomplices then cut off his head, and carried it to the Governor at Washington, which was the seat of the Territorial government. They received their reward. They, however, received another reward which they had not anticipated.

The proclamation of the governor had contained no promise whatever of pardon to any of the gang. These two men were immediately arrested, as robbers and murderers. They were tried, condemned and hung. The robber band, thus deprived of its leader and of two of its most desperate men, was broken up and the wretches dispersed, to fill up the measure of their iniquities in other regions.

But let us again cross the Rocky mountains, and contemplate some of the strange scenes of violence and blood which were occurring there. We have mentioned, that Kit Carson had been appointed, by Government Indian Commissioner. This gave him much satisfaction, for it was an office he felt perfectly competent to fill. It also was an evidence that, at last, his ability and services had been appreciated. He at once accepted the appointment and entered upon its duties.

He soon found the office no sinecure. The Apaches began to commit depredations upon the property of the settlers in the northern part of New Mexico. Some of the citizens fell a sacrifice to their barbarity. Mr. Carson at once sent Lieutenant Bell, a United States officer, with quite a force of dragoons, in pursuit of them. Although the red men were quite willing to scalp peaceful and unarmed citizens, when they found their own ranks torn and bleeding by the balls of their foes, and their chiefs biting the dust in the death agony, then courage gave place to terror, and flight became their resource.

Not long after, news came to Mr. Carson that another insurrection had appeared among the Apaches. They were encamped about twenty miles from Taos, upon quite a little ridge of mountains. Mr. Carson proceeded unattended, to their lodges, to meet the chiefs for a friendly talk. Having been among them for so many years, he was well known by nearly all the Rocky mountain tribes. Mr. Carson, by his gentle words and his personal influence, succeeded in pacifying them, and obtaining promises of friendly relations. Hardly had he left their lodges, when the treachery of the Indian became manifested in new crimes and barbarities. Carson, distrusting them, was not unprepared; but with a band of tried men inflicted such blows as were not soon forgotten.

Lieutenant Davidson was not long after this sent with a force of sixty United States Dragoons, to attack and dislodge an encampment in the mountains. They were all men who understood Indian character and warfare. Repairing to their fastnesses, they found the Indians well posted, and expecting a visit from the white men. Two hundred and more warriors were on the highest crags of the hills.

The Indian loves a *palaver* or talk; and the Lieutenant sent one or two men to endeavor to settle affairs thus amicably. But the savages, perceiving the inferior numbers of the white men, were not inclined to be communicative, or to listen to peaceful terms. Fight, blood, scalps, they thirsted for, and those they would have.

Perceiving that no pacific measures would avail, Lieutenant Davidson tried the effect of powder and lead. Many of the warriors fell dead, but the savages were so many and so fierce, that the odds were against the troops. In danger of being surrounded and of thus sacrificing the whole of his little army, Davidson decided to retreat down the mountains. Being hotly pursued he was obliged to contest every foot of his way. Trees, rocks, stumps were, as usual, Indian breastworks. With their unerring aim, they laid low twenty of the soldiers. Most of the other forty of Davidson's command were more or less severely wounded. Bravely the poor fellows fought, though unsuccessfully. They however escaped to Taos.

The people in Taos were much distressed, in learning of this disastrous termination of the battle. The next day they sent wagons to convey the remains of the fallen soldiers to a proper burial place. On reaching the spot, they found the inhuman savages had, as usual, mutilated the remains of every one, and had stripped them of their clothing. Not long after several Apaches appeared in the streets of a small Mexican settlement, clad in the garments of the slain dragoons, and afforded much amusement to the people by their grotesque appearance, and awkward endeavors to imitate military etiquette and courtesy.

As is always the case in every military disaster

Lieutenant Davidson's conduct has been assailed. But the evidence of the men of his command was, that his coolness in difficulty, his courage in danger, and his judgment in the retreat entitle him to credit, not censure. Mr. Carson does not justify the unkind accusations against him, but says:

"I am intimately acquainted with Lieutenant Davidson, and have been in engagements with him, where he has taken a prominent part, and can testify that he is as brave and discreet as it is possible for a man to be. Nearly every person engaged in, and who survived that day's bloody battle, has since told me, that his commanding officer never once sought shelter, but stood manfully exposed to the aim of the Indians, encouraging his men, and apparently unmindful of his own life. It was, however, in the retreat they say that he acted the most gallantly, for when every thing was going badly with the soldiers, he was as cool and collected as if under the guns of his fort. The only anxiety he exhibited was for the safety of his remaining men."

The Apaches left the region at once, wisely fearing retribution at the hand of their foes. Mr. Carson, in travelling homeward from Santa Fe, saw no trace of them. But their barbarities were not forgotten and new and more vigorous measures were taken to reduce them to submission.

Colonel Cook was appointed commander of this new expedition. Mr. Carson accompanied him. Forty Mexicans and several Pueblo Indians joined the party under the command of Mr. James H. Quinn. Passing on in a northerly direction, they came to a small river emptying into the Rio del Norte. This was a wild mountain stream, swollen into a foaming torrent, by melting snows and recent rains. But it must be crossed. It was perilous, for the bed was rocky and the current rapid.

Carson took the lead, piloting over party after party in safety. Arriving on the shore, they found a bold perpendicular bluff several hundred feet high confronting them. Pursuing a zigzag trail around the eminence, the top was at last reached, and they emerged into a rough country, broken by ravines and hills. Passing a day at a small Mexican village, they set off, the next morning, in search of the Apaches. Carson's keen, quick eye caught the trail, and rapidly they pursued their way for a couple of days, when they overtook the Indians, leisurely resting in one of their small villages. The horses of the savages were fresh, and remembering the death-dealing rifle of the white man, most of the Indians saved themselves by flight. The steeds of the soldiers were too weary for pursuit. Yet many Indian warriors were struck down by the bullets of their pursuers, and the horses and camp furniture of the savages, such as it was, fell into the hands of Colonel Cook's party. Mr. Carson describing these events says:

"To Captain Sykes, who commanded the infantry, is due the greatest amount of praise for the part he acted in our adventures. When his men were almost broken down with sore feet, long and difficult marches, want of provisions, the coldness of the weather, and with their clothing nearly worn out, and when they were on the point of giving up in despair, they were prevented from so doing by witnessing the noble example set them by their captain. He showed them what a soldier's duty really was, and this so touched their pride that they hobbled álong as if determined to follow him until death relieved them from their sufferings.

"Although this officer had a riding animal at his disposal, yet never for once did he mount him; but instead lent the horse to some deserving soldier who was on the point of succumbing to overwork. When the Indian village was discovered, he cheered his men from a limping walk into a sort of run, and dashing through a swollen mountain stream, which was nearly up to their armpits, and full of floating ice, he was, with his company, the foremost in the attack."

Night put a stop to the pursuit. The next morning, at an early hour, Colonel Cook's dragoons were again in motion, following, under the guidance of Mr. Carson, the fresh trail of the routed Indians. On and still on they pressed for many weary leagues, through valleys and over snow-clad mountains, until they found that it was impossible to overtake the red men. The sagacious Indians broke up their party into small squads of two and three and scattered in all directions. To continue the pursuit would be like chasing "a flea upon the mountains."

The Indians had manifested a great deal, not of cunning only, but of intelligence in their flight. It was their manifest object to lead their pursuers through the most difficult paths, that both men and horses might be worn out by the ruggedness of the way. Very often they would pursue a route so circuitous, through wild gorges and over mountain torrents, that Colonel Cook would often find himself bivouacking at night, but a short distance from the spot which he had left in the morning. The Indians were perfectly familiar with the country and could travel with much greater ease than could the white men.

Colonel Cook, finding that nothing could be accomplished by the further continuance of the pursuit, turned back and sought a refuge for his soldiers from the toils and hardships of their campaign, in the little Mexican town of Abiguire, about sixty miles northwest from Sante Fè, on a tributary of the Rio del Norte.

On his march back, Colonel Cook had encountered and captured an Indian warrior, whom he supposed to be one of the hostile Apaches. The Indian was deprived of his horse and arms, and treated as a captive. He made his escape. Afterwards it was learned that he belonged to the friendly Utah tribe. Colonel Cook, regretting the mistake, and fearing that it might induce the Utahs to join the Apaches, very wisely decided to do his duty, and make an apology and reparation.

Kit Carson was, of course, employed as the ambassador of peace. He sent an Indian runner to the principal village of the Utahs, with the request that their chief would hold a council with him. They all knew him, loved him, and familiarly called him "Father Kit."

The council met, Mr. Carson explained the mistake and expressed the deepest regret, that through ignorance, one of their friendly braves had been captured, and treated like an enemy. He assured them of his readiness to make ample reparation for the wrong.

"My countrymen," he said, "do not wish to do

you any injury. They hope that you will overlook this accident. They do not ask this through fear. The warriors of the Utah are but a handful, when compared with those of their Great Father. But they wish to live with you as brothers. The country is large enough for both."

The Indians seemed ever ready to listen to reason. They were satisfied with the explanation, and declared that their hearts were no longer inimical to their pale face brothers. Thus another Indian war was averted. Had the Indians always been treated with this spirit of justice and conciliation, humanity would have been saved from innumerable woes.

# CHAPTER XVIII.

## *The Last Days of Kit Carson.*

**The** Hunting Party.—Profits of Sheep Raising.—Governmental Appointment.—Carson's Talk with the Apaches.—His Home in Taos.—His Character.—Death of Christopher Carson.

WE left Mr. Carson at his farm in Razado. After a short time he organized a pleasure hunting-party of eighteen of his most highly esteemed companions of former years. It was unanimously voted that the excursion should not be one of boy's play but of man's. It was Carson's last trapping excursion. Each trapper felt that he was bidding farewell to the streams and valleys, where in past years, he had encountered so many exciting adventures.

"The boldest and one of the longest routes, known to their experienced footsteps, was selected. It comprised many of the mighty rivers of the Rocky mountains, every one of which was almost a hunting ground by itself. Onward, over the wild and broad plains, this band of stalwart men, brave and kindred spirits, dashed. They soon put several miles between them and the comfortable firesides of Razado.

"In a short time the well remembered waters of the South Platte were descried. Their practiced eyes soon discovered the oft noted "signs of the beaver." The beaver had increased in great numbers. The party continued working down this stream, through the plains of Laramie to the New Park; and thence on to the Old Park. They trapped a large number of their old streams, until finally the expedition was terminated on the Arkansas river. The hunt proved very successful. With a large stock of furs, they returned in safety to Razado, via the Raton mountains, which are spurs of the great Rocky chain."

This expedition occupied several months. Mr. Carson now devoted himself assiduously to farming, and especially to raising flocks and herds. In August, 1853, he drove, aided by many well armed attendants, a flock of six thousand five hundred sheep to California, where he sold them for five dollars and fifty cents a head. His knowledge of the country was such, that he was enabled to follow a route which gave them good pasturage all the way.

At San Francisco, Kit Carson found himself an object of universal attention. His renown had preceded him. The steamboats gave him a free pass,

All places of amusement were open to him. Where-ever he went he was pointed out as the man to whom California was under the greatest obligations. Still he retained his modesty and integrity unsullied. Soon after his return to Razado, he received the unexpected and very gratifying intelligence, that he had been appointed by the United States Government, Indian Agent.

The duties of this difficult and responsible office he performed with remarkable wisdom and success. Whenever his counsel was followed it, was attended with the desired results. Whenever it was rejected disaster was sure to ensue. His knowledge of Indian customs was such, that more than once he presented himself entirely alone at the council fire of exasperated warriors; and urged upon them peace. On one of these occasions he learned that an angry band of Apache warriors were encamped among the mountains, but about fifty miles from his home. He knew the chiefs. He was familiar with their language. Though he knew that they were in a state of great exasperation, and that they were preparing to enter upon the war-path, he mounted his horse and rode thither, without even an attendant. The chiefs received him with sullen looks; but they listened patiently to his speech.

"The course you are pursuing," said he, "will lead

to your inevitable and total destruction. Your tribe will be exterminated. Your Great Father has thousands upon thousands of soldiers. He can easily replace those who fall in battle. It is not so with you. When your warriors are killed, you have no others to place in their moccasins. You must wait for the children to grow up.

"Your Great Father loves his children. He wishes to give you rich presents. I am his servant to bring those presents to you. We wish to live in peace, that we may help one another."

This conciliatory speech softened their hearts for a time, and they all, with seeming cordiality, came forward and professed friendship. The great difficulty, in our intercourse with the Indians, has been that the wilderness has been filled with miserable vagabonds, who were ever perpetrating innumerable outrages, robbing them, and treating them in all respects, in the most shameless manner. Even civilized men, in war, will often retaliate, by punishing the innocent for the crimes of the guilty. It is not strange that untutored Indians, having received atrocious wrongs from one band of white men, should wreak their vengeance on the next band whom they chanced to encounter.

Mr. Carson, in addition to his farm at Razada, had what may be called his city residence in the straggling old town of Taos. It is said that a traveller upon entering these crooked streets, lined with one story buildings of sun-baked bricks, is reminded of a number of brick-kilns, previous to being burnt, all huddled together without any regard to order. As in all Spanish towns, there is a large public square in the centre.

Mr. Carson's house faced this square on the west side. Though but one story in height, it spread over a large extent of ground. It was one of the largest and most commodious houses in the place. Every body who went to Taos, Indians as well as white men, felt bound to call upon " Father Kit," as he was familiarly called. To the Indian, particularly, he was ever a true friend and benefactor. He knew, as no other man knew, how terrible his wrongs,—not from the government,—but from the vagabond desperadoes of the wilderness. Never was his patience exhausted by their long visits, and never was he weary of listening to their harangues. It has ever been with him a constant effort to warn them against the use of intoxicating drink—that " fire water" which has so long been consuming the Indian, body and soul.

Whenever the government had any important or delicate mission to preform among the Indians, the services of Mr. Carson were sure to be called into requisition. Thus he entered upon the evening of his days, honored and beloved by all who knew him. These peaceful hours were probably the happiest of his life. We have no detailed account of his last sickness and death. He breathed his last at Fort Lyon, in Colorado, on the twenty-third of May, 1868, in the sixtieth year of his age. The immediate cause of his death, was an aneurism of an artery in the neck. Thus passed away one of the most illustrious of the "Pioneers and Patriots" of America. His name deserves to be held in perpetual remembrance.

## CHAPTER XIX.

*The Last Hours of Kit Carson.*

THE following letter, received since the publication of the first edition, gives an interesting account of the last hours of Mr. Carson from the physician who was with him when he died.

"FORT WADSWORTH,
NEW YORK HARBOR,
*January, 7th,* 1874.

"MR. JOHN S. C. ABBOTT,
FAIRHAVEN, CONN.

"*Dear Sir:*—

"I have just read your interesting life of Kit Carson, and write to give you a short account of his last sickness and death. I first met him at the house of a mutual friend, not far from Fort Lyon, C. T., late in the Fall of 1867. He had then recently left the service of the U. S., having been colonel of a regiment of New-Mexican volunteers during the war of the rebellion.

"As I was a successful amateur trapper, he threw off all reserve, and greeted me with more than usual warmth, saying, 'the happiest days of my life were spent in trapping.' He gave me many practical hints on trapping and hunting.

"He was then complaining of a pain in his chest, the origin of which he attributed to a fall received in 1860. It happened while he was descending a mountain. The declivity was so steep that he led his horse by the lariat, intending, if the horse fell to throw it from him.

"The horse did fall, and although he let go the lariat, it caught him and carried him a number of feet, and severely bruised him.

"In the Spring of 1868, he took charge of a party of Ute Indians, and accompanied them to Washington and other cities, going as far east as Boston. He consulted a number of physicians while on the trip.

"It was a great tax on his failing strength to make this journey; but he was ever ready to promote the welfare of the Utes, who regarded him in the light of a father.

"I saw him in April, 1868. His disease, aneurism of the aorta, had progressed rapidly; and the tumor pressing on the pneumo-gastric nerves and trachea, caused frequent spasms of the bronchial tubes which were exceedingly distressing.

"On the 27th of April, Mrs. Carson died very suddenly, leaving seven children, the youngest only two weeks old. Mrs. Carson was tall and spare, and had evidently been a very handsome woman; she was thirty-eight years old at the time of her death, and he informed me that they had been married twenty-five years. Her sudden death had a very depressing effect upon him.

"I called frequently to see him; and as he was living on the south side of the Arkansas River five miles from Fort Lyon where I was stationed, and the Spring rise coming on, making the fording difficult, I suggested that he be brought to my quarters, which was done on the 14th day of May.

"This enabled me to make his condition much more comfortable. In the interval of his paroxysms, he beguiled the time by relating past experiences. I read Dr. Peters' book, with the hero for my auditor; from time to time, he would comment on the incidents of his eventful life.

"It was wonderful to read of the stirring scenes, thrilling deeds, and narrow escapes, and then look at the quiet, modest, retiring, but dignified little man who had done so much.

"You are perfectly correct in describing Carson as a gentleman. He was one of nature's noblemen—a true man in all that consitutes manhood—pure—honorable—truthful—sincere—of noble impulses, a true knight-errant ever ready to defend the weak against the strong, without reward other than his own conscience.

"Carson had great contempt for noisy braggarts and shams of every sort.

"His disease rapidly progressed and he calmly contemplated his approaching death. Several times he repeated the remark, 'If it was not for this,' pointing to his chest; 'I might live to be a hundred years old.'

"I explained to him the probable mode of termination of his disease: 'that he might die from suffocation or more probably the aneurism would burst and cause death by hemorrhage. He expressed a decided preference for the latter mode. His attacks of dyspnœa were horrible, threatening immediate dissolution. I was compelled to give chloroform to relieve him, at considerable risk of hastening a fatal result; but he begged me not to let him suffer such tortures, and if I killed him by chloroform while attempting relief, it would be much better than death by suffocation.

"Once, he remarked: 'What am I to do, I can't get along without a doctor?'

"I replied, 'I'll take care of you.'

"He, smiling, said, 'You must think I am not going to live long.'

"The night preceding death he spent more comfortably than he had for days before. He was obliged to sit up nearly all the time. He coughed up a slight amount of blood during the night, and a very little in the forenoon.

"In the afternoon, while I was lying down on his bed and he was listening to Mr Sherrick, he suddenly called out 'Doctor, Compadre, Adios!'

"I sprang to him and seeing a gush of blood pouring from his mouth, remarked, 'this is the last of the general;' I supported his forehead on my hand, while death speedily closed the scene.

"The aneurism had ruptured into the trachea Death took place at 4. 25 P. M., May 23rd 1868.

Mr. Carson was a small man not over five feet six inches tall, with gray eyes, light-brown hair tinged with gray; his head was large; forehead high and broad; his nose somewhat *retroussé*. He had a good broad chest and a compact form. He had been a remarkably quick active man and what he lacked in strength, he made up in agility. It is related of him, that while he was in command of his regiment and on a campaign against the Navajo Indians, he would leave camp very early each morning, taking his Ute Indian scouts, and let his lieutenant-colonel take charge of the regiment; before the command would have time to come up with the fugitive enemy, Carson and his Utes had finished the fighting.

"I am under the impression that the Navajo nation, numbering 8,000 or 10,000 people were so severely pressed by Kit Carson, that they surrendered to him, and were put on a government reservation, where they remained under military control, for several years. Within the last three years they have been permitted to return to the country formerly occupied by them; but I am not positive of the above.

"Carson was made a brigadier-general of volunteers by brevet, at the close of the rebellion.

"Shortly after coming to my quarters he made his will, and left property to the value of seven thousand dollars to his children.

"No post-mortem was made. The pulse at the right radial artery was very indistinct, while the left continued good.

"I have been thus minute, thinking that while writing his life, you had grown to love him, as all who knew him certainly cherished great affection for him.

"Yours Truly,
"H. R. TILTON,
"*Ass't Surgeon U. S. Army.*

THE END.

www.ingramcontent.com/pod-product-compliance
Lightning Source LLC
LaVergne TN
LVHW010145110826
845151LV00002B/434

* 9 7 8 1 4 2 5 5 3 7 3 4 0 *